60-4

D0906215

PLOTS AND CHARACTERS
IN THE FICTION OF
THEODORE DREISER

THE PLOTS AND CHARACTERS SERIES

Robert L. Gale
General Editor

GERBER, Philip L. **Plots and characters in the fiction of Theodore Dreiser.** Archon, 1977. 153p 76-54792. 12.50 ISBN 0-208-01490-X. C.I.P.

This book will serve both the specialist and the general reader who wants a sense of Dreiser's total work before settling on a book or two to read. There are clear, informative outlines of all the fiction, including the short stories, that Dreiser published in book form between 1900 and 1947. There is also a separate section that lists alphabetically all the significant characters in these works. When one considers that *An American tragedy* alone contains nearly 180 such characters, the book's reason for being becomes apparent. Moreover, while one might anticipate the utility of this sort of guide, rarely do handbooks have any critical value. But Gerber's brief preface happens to be one of the most insightful general commentaries on Dreiser to appear for some time. Gerber, of course, is suited to his task: he is a noted Dreiser specialist who writes with grace. His *Theodore Dreiser* (CHOICE, Jul.-Aug. 1964) is a standard critical text, and his more recent edition of Dreiser's Cowperwood trilogy is a major contribution to the field. Surprisingly for such a careful scholar, there are a few factual mistakes: Gerber has Dreiser marrying Sara White in November 1898, not, as it should be, on December 28, 1898; and he says Dreiser began working on *Jennie*

Continued

GERBER

Gerhardt in the 1907–09 period, while in fact over thirty chapters of the novel had been completed by the end of 1901. But these are relatively minor blemishes in a book whose function, after all, is to be useful, not scholarly. Recommended for all academic libraries.

PLOTS AND CHARACTERS
IN THE FICTION OF
THEODORE DREISER

Philip L. Gerber

Archon Books
Dawson

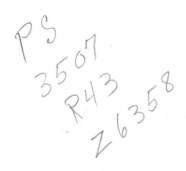

©Philip L. Gerber 1977
First Published in 1977

All rights reserved. No part of this publication may be reproduced, stored in a retrieval system, or transmitted, in any form or by any means, electronic, mechanical photocopying, recording, or otherwise without the permission of the publishers:

Archon Books, The Shoe String Press Inc
995 Sherman Avenue, Hamden, Connecticut 06514 USA
Wm Dawson & Sons Ltd, Cannon House
Folkestone, Kent, England

Library of Congress Cataloging in Publication Data

Gerber, Philip L.
    Plots and characters in the fiction of Theodore Dreiser.

    (The Plots and characters series)
    Bibliography: p.
    1. Dreiser, Theodore, 1871-1945—Plots.   2. Dreiser, Theodore, 1871-1945—Characters. I. Title.
PS3507.R55Z6358   813'.5'2   76-54792

Archon   ISBN 0-208-01490-X
Dawson   ISBN 0 7129 0758 0

Printed in the United States of America

American literature is nicely landscaped with foothills, but the mountain peaks are few and rare and widely scattered. Dreiser is one of the highest peaks, and on a clear day can be seen around the world.

Norman Corwin

05060

CONTENTS

PREFACE

PREFACE

For the reader interested in Theodore Dreiser and his works this volume may serve a variety of needs. One may wish to become acquainted with the broad outlines of one of Dreiser's bulky novels before undertaking the book itself, or he may hope merely to reacquaint himself with details of action in a story read previously but dimmed in the memory since. Having enjoyed one or another of Dreiser's novels, a reader may wish to compare the outline of its plot with those of other novels by the same author. Or, one who has studied the novels may without undue effort use the résumés of the shorter fiction as a means of perceiving parallels with the longer works.

In keeping with their breadth, Dreiser's novels teem with people. *An American Tragedy* alone encompasses nearly 180 individuals who play roles of some significance, *The Titan* not many less than that number. It is no simple matter to keep fresh in mind the names of all Dreiser's characters, even those from a single book. Here the names of characters may easily be checked for spelling or for identification, or the lists may be used for other purposes required by a particular reader. More significant uses for this volume may be cited, their applicability limited only by a reader's degree of literary sophistication or by an interest in Dreiser and knowledge of the man's work.

When Dreiser died in 1945 and one of his obituaries compared the loss to receiving news that a familiar headland of the continent had slid into the sea and vanished, it not only was a recognition of the near half-century that the novelist had been a dominant, and often controversial, figure, but it also took note of the solid position Dreiser had established for himself in American letters. Now, more than thirty years since that death, Dreiser's position in literary history is no less secure. Indeed, considering the army of novelists come and gone in the interim, his reputation is perhaps even more solidly grounded now than it was in an earlier day.

On an afternoon in the 1800s, as a boy in his earliest teens, Dreiser first witnessed the mile upon mile of raw streets marked

out upon Chicago's bare prairie well in advance of the inevitable
influx of population. From that day he understood in his bones
that city life held the key to the American future. In his books,
almost without an exception, his characters are compelled to con-
tend with the difficult complexity and impersonalism of urban life.
He comprehended early that America was rushing headlong into
a time when industry would all but obliterate an older, agricultural-
ly centered society. The triumph of capitalism was imminent; the
new day would be known by its guiding principle, profit, and would
be dominated by its characteristic invention, the industrial millionaire.

As reflected in Dreiser's fiction, life in the new era assumes an
unmistakable aura of practicality and shapes itself into a breathing
illustration of Turgot's maxim that life at bottom is a fact of eco-
nomics. The industrial era produces no less than a new way of
life. Paralleling the growth of the cities, money becomes solidly
fixed as the single conceivable medium of exchange, and all of
Dreiser's people have good reason to be obsessed with dollars and
cents. The nature and precise amount of one's income becomes a
matter of central importance to the individual citizen, for the
course of one's existence fluctuates in harmony with the least
variation in one's "cash flow."

In the modern world the mass media assume a special promi-
nence, one signaled in Dreiser's fiction by the rise of the newspaper (the novelist himself, like other writers of his time, such as
Stephen Crane and Willa Cather, began his career as a reporter
and graduated from printer's ink to literature). In keeping with
the phenomena of mass media apparent to us in this latter day,
the daily papers in Dreiser's stories tend not only to reflect the
life milling around them but also to shape and even to mold it.
A reader of *Jennie Gerhardt*, for instance, notes that Jennie's romance with Lester Kane, idyllic so long as it remains a strictly
private affair, is destroyed once the newspapers publicize it with
photographs and lurid headlines: *This Millionaire Fell in Love with This
Lady's Maid*. And in *The Titan* the powerful financier Frank Algernon
Cowperwood comes to ruin largely as a result of the vendetta
maintained against him by local editors. Even a cursory study of
the plots of Dreiser's short stories reveals the extent to which he
recognized the centrality of the newspaper reporter and used him
as a focus in creating fiction.

In the urban-industrial universe the nature of occupations is altered. It is not by accident that Dreiser arranges for the heroine of *Sister Carrie* to inaugurate her independent working career as the lowliest worker sewing shoes on a rudimentary form of what would evolve into the modern assembly line. And to know that Carrie Meeber eventually achieves fame and fortune as a popularly acclaimed star of the entertainment sphere is to recognize that Dreiser understood another national trait which would become fully apparent only in later times: Americans were eager to shower disproportionate rewards upon those who managed to divert them from the dispiriting grind of daily routine.

One use of a book which summarizes Dreiser's plots in a discrete group is that it facilitates identification of trends such as those just illustrated. And one can see also that Dreiser recognized other patterns which were to become part and parcel of the "American way." An instance is the emergent mobility of the populace. As rapidly as the machine age could manage to arrange for it, unrestricted freedom of movement was opened to all, not merely as a convenience or luxury, but because the system depended upon getting things and people from place to place with speed and precision—and of course because transportation systems were good moneymakers. One of Dreiser's men, Frank Algernon Cowperwood in *The Titan*, makes a fortune on streetcars; but travel became the thing for everyone, whether one merely went from one part of Chicago to another on a Cowperwood trolley, moved intercontinentally aboard a luxury liner, invading Europe to buy up the best of its art treasures as Frank Cowperwood does, or clung as a transient to a freight train as the fugitive Clyde Griffiths makes his way from Kansas City to Chicago in *An American Tragedy*.

The incessant changes of address experienced by Carrie Meeber, Jennie Gerhardt, and others are symptomatic of all Dreiser's people: without roots, forever forced to adapt to new places, new populations, new conditions. His restless Americans stand in the vanguard of the phenomenon only recently defined as "future shock." Too much is occurring too soon; men can scarcely keep their balance in the swift rush of events. Carrie Meeber almost before she knows it is swept off to Montreal and then to New York with her embezzler-lover; Jennie Gerhardt and Lester Kane attempt to protect the secrecy of their illicit liaison by flitting from suburb to suburb in quest of privacy; so trivial an event as an automobile accident sends Clyde Griffiths from Kansas City to Chicago, and from there a chance meeting with an uncle takes him to upstate

New York; even the titanic Frank Cowperwood finds his empire washing from beneath his boots when an unanticipated tide of civic reform engulfs Chicago. Dreiser's novels being the lengthy affairs they are, summaries such as those provided here allow for an ease of comparison, one to another, not readily achieved otherwise.

It is undeniable that Dreiser's spontaneous immersion in the modern spirit, a genuine love for his own time reflected on every page of his books, has helped the novels to achieve their enviable longevity. But that is hardly the sole reason for the novelist's power to endure. Other men have written stories as extended and as thoroughly imbued with the modern, both in spirit and in *mise-en-scène*. But Dreiser invariably provides what few other writers have been capable of: a consistent and compelling thematic stance. Dreiser chanced along just at the critical juncture in history when the age-old verities, long under siege, seemed in process of receiving the *coup de grace* delivered by nineteenth-century science. He was born into a conventionally religious family but found himself unable to accept its premises, particularly when their repudiation seemed inherent in every new direction then being taken by a rapidly altering social order.

Thus Dreiser observed his own life develop into a persistent but largely futile search for some new authority capable of replacing that which had been lost. Charles Darwin was among the first of his new gods, then Herbert Spencer, like Darwin a champion of the evolutionary principle, who impressed Dreiser with his persuasive image of man standing alone and fragile at the mercy of immense universal forces. Industrialism appeared to foster a brutal individualistic spirit much akin to that which was central to Darwin's jungle world. One's survival was largely up to oneself. Endowed with the right qualities, a man might become a commanding figure, even a multimillionaire. But, in a capricious world he might as easily end as a derelict in a breadline, commit suicide, and his corpse be consigned to Potter's Field. In his novels Dreiser described both extremes. It was a frightening challenge, this new freedom to succeed mightily—or to fail. When the human individual was placed in such straits, the primacy of self-interest was clearly indicated, and most of Dreiser's moderns are kept too busy looking out for themselves to worry much about being their brother's keeper.

Science and pseudoscience alike had their effects on Theodore

Dreiser in his search for the meaning of what he called "the way life has organized itself." At one time he was much attracted by Elmer Gates, the biopsychologist, and by the mind-building panacea which Gates called "psychurgy"; at another moment he became a devotee of the laboratory scientist Jacques Loeb, whose experiments with tropism in plant life promised to answer deep questions about the conduct of the human species. At every stage of his life Dreiser continued to take note of superstitious occurrences and to consult spiritualists and clairvoyants. In his own embrace of one potential answer after another Dreiser prefigured the quandary of modern man. Old coherences lost, society appeared to be at the mercy of any sudden enthusiasm for a cure-all, whether it be economic, political, religious, or philosophical.

A telling feature of the modern quest for authority has been its apparent failure to locate any truly persuasive explanation for the enigma we call life. Hence the trauma of perpetual search has been made inevitable. However enthusiastic might be Dreiser's personal conversion to this or that philosophical answer, all explanations sooner or later failed, leaving him face to face with the great riddle. And so the question of life's import itself became his stance. Asked in his middle years for a statement of his life-philosophy, he described earthly existence as "a welter of inscrutable forces" in which was trapped each "utterly infinitesimal" human being: "I catch no meaning from all I have seen, and pass quite as I came, confused and dismayed."

Ordinarily an admission of this nature might be denigrated or even brushed aside entirely as constituting no philosophy at all; but as luck would have it, Dreiser found himself lodged in a mainstream of twentieth-century indecision. His vision of the human being stranded by himself in a precarious field dark with mystery was something that modern man could easily respond to. His personal experience found its parallel in an ever-increasing horde of individual lives. His novels, without any contrivance on his part, were able to capitalize upon this sense of estrangement; for after all else has been said, what remains in the books is a tableau of empathic force: a figure solitary, often beleaguered, invariably bewildered. Some examples: Carrie Meeber amazed at the unpredictable turn of events which has showered her with fame and fortune; Jennie Gerhardt pondering the obscure significance of her lonely years of giving; Frank Cowperwood discovering that even a colossus is no more than a pygmy in the universal scheme of things; Clyde Griffiths unable to comprehend whether he has or has not committed murder, and why; Solon Barnes in *The Bulwark* disoriented at the abject failure of all his well-laid plans. Gathered in one place, these plots show themselves to be but variations upon a single major story, that of the human individual ineffectually struggling against hostile forces and impotent even to comprehend them.

Dreiser was a natural-born novelist. Being a genuine man of letters as well, he gave every major form a try, from the essay to the drama, the poem to the story, but he was enduringly successful and characteristically himself only with long prose fiction. His self-evaluation, that for his best work he required a large canvas as well as a huge enthusiasm, was made early in his career and was precisely to the point. What mattered to him first and last was never the single moment, however illuminated or emotionally heightened, which became sacred to the modern writer of short stories. It was his nature instead to aim for the accretive impact which comes from reporting upon a total life. For Dreiser there were no epiphanies. Rather, an individual learned slowly and painfully by enduring long years of living, while all the time existence rained its blows. At last—and perhaps against his will—the individual, by nature a creature saturated with illusion, could not escape glimpsing a part of the bitter truth concerning life. Hence Dreiser's plots generally run the full cycle from cradle to crypt.

Dreiser's short stories, on the other hand, more often than not prove to be an embarrassment. Eventually he gave up writing them entirely and left many unfinished, unpublished or uncollected. Included in this volume are no stories beyond those which Dreiser himself saw fit to collect in enduring form in his volumes *Free* and *Chains*. Notwithstanding the risk of being thought arbitrary, one might wish to be even more selective in editing. However, Dreiser in his rare, more successful efforts in the short form does manage to produce something resembling the impact made by his novels. His best stories succeed in conveying the familiar stark picture of a human being isolated, unprotected, and subject to the hostility, or at best to the indifference, of a stony universe where fierce winds blow. In such cases Dreiser's tendency is to work toward explicit statements which parallel the themes upon which his novels are grounded:

"Life was so deceptive; it used and then tossed one aside."
                                                        ("The Victor")

"Life seemed so sad, so strange, so mysterious, so inexpli-
cable."
                                                        ("Nigger Jeff")

"One of the disturbing things about all this was the iron truth
which it had driven home, namely that Nature . . . cared
no whit for him or for any man or woman."
                                                        ("Free")

There was not much of the poet in Dreiser; yet his fiction on occasion does achieve an image whose effect is to display the essence of his thought. One memorable instance occurs in "The
Old Neighborhood," wherein by means of a slaughterhouse image
he defines the "automatic and unconsciously cruel" nature of life:
"One's disposition drove one on so, shutting and bolting doors
behind one, driving one on and on like a harried steer up a narrow
runway to one's fate."
The roster of characters in this volume reflects Dreiser's position as the first major American writer to come from other than
Anglo-Saxon derivation. His appearance in 1900 opened the door
for the vast range of literary names we recognize today, from Dos
Passos to Steinbeck to Saroyan to Nabokov to Vonnegut. In Dreiser's fiction the immigrant peoples, for the first time in our literature, take on a vast importance. The reader regularly encounters
ethnic tags that run the full gamut. Gerecht, Haeckelheimer,
McGlathery, Nikoforitch, Nowack, Petkanis, Pinski, Pitti, Rogaum,
Rubenstein, Schlict, Swanson, Tuckerman, and Zang are examples; but they only scratch the surface of Dreiser's fictional
census. Generally these people represent the American pro-
letariat, recently arrived on these shores; or else, like the Irish
politicians Tierney and Kerrigan in *The Titan*, they have risen from
the ranks, of which Dreiser invariably is aware and which he always
takes pains to make clear. On the other hand, British Isle patronym-
ics are reserved by and large for the *de facto* aristocracy and
ordinarily indicate those who hold status of a social or economic
nature: Hull, MacDonald, Merrill, Sledd, Waltham, Williams.
A reader interested in further implications cast by Dreiser's use
of names will be struck at once by the large number of aliases

employed by his characters. This fact becomes considerably more obvious when characters are isolated from plots and identified methodically. The prevalence of the alias is one more indication that those who gain Dreiser's attention include a desperate corps compelled by conditions to operate *sub rosa*, beyond the clutches of the powerful American respectability cult. One might consider here the range of pseudonyms adopted by Jennie Gerhardt in her search for anonymity or those employed by George Hurstwood as he attempts to elude the law. Clyde Griffiths alone uses a half-dozen aliases in his abortive effort to commit the perfect murder. Other motives for a change of name would include the evolving style of the theatrical world as it attempts to ape the dominant social groups by cloaking lowly origins. Thus, just as Dreiser's own brother Paul found it advantageous to change his name to Dresser in order to succeed in the musical-comedy world, Carrie Meeber on her way to stardom undergoes a similar metamorphosis, from which she emerges as Carrie Madenda.

Mindful that the versatility of the human brain will prompt it eventually to make demands upon this handbook which are presently not anticipated, I hope that the data gathered here may prove equal to the occasion. It should be noted that in listing the characters of Dreiser's fiction I have silently omitted any person who is merely named in passing and who remains a name only, without serving any active function in a plot. I wish to thank Mr. Harold J. Dies of The Dreiser Trust for permission to summarize those works still in copyright; and I must also thank Professor Robert L. Gale, editor of this series, for his generous and valuable guidance in preparing the manuscript.

Philip L. Gerber

State University of New York
Brockport, New York

CHRONOLOGY

1871   Theodore Dreiser born August 27 in Terre Haute, Indiana, son of John Paul Dreiser, immigrant German miller, and Sarah Schanab Dreiser.

1879-84   Frequent moves of Dreiser family occasioned by ill health and unemployment of John Paul Dreiser; temporary residences in Vincennes, Sullivan, and Evansville, Indiana; periodic separation of family members.

1884   Dreiser family settles temporarily in Chicago.

1884-86   Dreiser family members separate once again; Theodore goes with mother to live in Warsaw, Indiana; is taught in high school by Miss Mildred Fielding.

1886   Returns to Chicago on his own at age sixteen.

1886-89   Employed in unskilled jobs in Chicago. Dreiser family regroups in that city.

1889-90   Mildred Fielding sponsors his only college training, freshman year at Indiana University, Bloomington.

1890   Sarah Schanab Dreiser dies, November 14. Dreiser family disperses permanently. Theodore begins journalistic career on Chicago *Globe*. Moves to St. Louis, November, to work for *Globe-Democrat*, subsequently for *Republic*.

1893   Assigned by *Republic* to escort trainload of contest winners to World's Columbian Exposition, Chicago; meets future wife, Sara White, known as "Jug." Older brother Paul Dresser (né Dreiser) visits, encourages quest for fame and fortune in New York.

1894   Leaves St. Louis for New York, via Toledo, Cleveland, Buffalo, Pittsburgh. Works as reporter for Pittsburgh *Dispatch*. At The Allegheny Free Library discovers the novels of Honoré de Balzac and *First Principles* of Herbert Spencer. Visits Paul in New York; determines to complete move there as rapidly as possible.

1895   New York career begins. Works for Pulitzer's *World*. Paul aids in establishing periodical *Every Month*, which he edits.

1896-99   Free-lance writing for Sunday supplements and magazines such as *Ainslee's*. Writes extended series of articles based upon interviews for Orison Swett Marden's *Success*. His name becomes known in journalistic circles.

1898   Marries Jug White, November.

1899   Spends summer months in home of friend Arthur Henry, Maumee, Ohio; both men write fiction. Begins *Sister Carrie*, based upon his sisters' lives.

1900   *Sister Carrie* published by Doubleday, Page & Co. after the firm has attempted without success to renege on its contract. Notices are mixed, sales miniscule.

1901   *Sister Carrie* published in England by Heinemann, with greater success, initiating Dreiser's career in England.
"McEwen of the Shining Slave Makers" (as "The Shining Slave Makers") (1918)*
"Nigger Jeff" (1918)
"Old Rogaum and His Theresa" (as "Butcher Rogaum's Door") (1918)
"When the Old Century Was New" (1918)

1901-03   Experiences nervous collapse; while recuperating spends time at William Muldoon's health camp, works as day laborer on railroad crew.

1904   Regains health. Becomes fiction editor, July, for Street and Smith pulp-novel factory, New York.

1905   Rises in magazine-editing field. Becomes editor of *Smith's Magazine*, April. Death in New York, December, of C. T. Yerkes, Jr., whose life is to supply pattern for novels *The Financier, The Titan, The Stoic*.

1906   Becomes editor of *Broadway Magazine*, April. July-December, Grace Brown murder, Chester Gillette trial, later to supply pattern for novel *An American Tragedy*.

1907   *Sister Carrie* republished by B. W. Dodge, May, reviving career as novelist. Assumes directorship of Butterick Corporation, becomes editor of *Butterick* magazine.

1907-09   Great success as magazine editor; begins friendship with critic H. L. Mencken; begins work on novel *Jennie Gerhardt*.

*Dates within parentheses indicate first book publication.

1909   "The Cruise of the 'Idlewild'" (1918)

1910   Falls in love with Thelma Cudlipp, eighteen; on her
        account loses position with Butterick Corporation.
        Separates from Sara White Dreiser. Goes into free-
        lance writing. Begins autobiographical novel *The
        "Genius"*; engages in research on C. T. Yerkes, Jr., for
        novel *The Financier*.

1911   *Jennie Gerhardt*, novel based upon his sisters' lives, ac-
        cepted by Harper and Brothers, April; published,
        November. Travels to Europe with Grant Richards,
        British publisher, ostensibly to research overseas
        career of Yerkes for *The Financier*, already underway.

1912   Returns from Europe, April, to complete *The Financier*.
        Agreement with Harper to extend this novel into
        three-volume *Trilogy of Desire*. Part I, *The Financier*,
        published, October. Begins travel book based on
        European trip. Travels to Chicago, December, to
        research Part II, *A Trilogy of Desire*, under title *The
        Titan*.

1913   Returns from Chicago, February. Completes *A Traveler
        at Forty*; published by Century Company, November.
        Completes *The Titan*.

1914   Travels to Chicago, March; Harper rejects *The Titan*
        after printing 8500 copies. Transfers to John Lane
        Company. Lane publishes *The Titan*, May. Outbreak
        of World War I places the pro-German Dreiser and
        Mencken under tensions which cement their friend-
        ship.

1915   Travels to Midwest by automobile with illustrator
        Franklin Booth, August, to research book of In-
        diana reminiscences. John Lane publishes *The "Genius,"*
        October. Stuart P. Sherman publishes first major
        anti-Dreiser essay, "The Naturalism of Mr. Dreiser,"
        in *The Nation*.

1916   Lane publishes *Plays of the Natural and the Supernatural*, six
        one-act dramas; withdraws *The "Genius"* from market
        after New York Society for the Suppression of Vice
        bans it as immoral. Indiana book, *A Hoosier Holiday*,
        published.
        "The Lost Phoebe" (1918)

1917   Attempts without success to reinstate *The "Genius."*

Prolific writing of essays, plays, short stories. Mencken replies to Sherman attack with pro-Dreiser essay, "The Dreiser Bugaboo," in *The Seven Arts*.

"Married" (1918)

1918   Transfers to Boni & Liveright. Publishes *Free and Other Stories, The Hand of the Potter* (drama), *Twelve Men* (sketches).

"Free"
"The Old Neighborhood" (1927)
"The Second Choice"
"A Story of Stories"
"Will You Walk into My Parlor?"

1919   "Chains" (as "Love") (1927)
"The Hand" (1927)
"Sanctuary" (1927)

1919-22   First encounters Helen Richardson, long-time companion and eventual wife. Residence in Hollywood, where Helen plays in motion pictures. Publishes *Hey Rub-A-Dub-Dub* (philosophical essays, 1920); *A Book About Myself* (autobiography, 1922). Begins novel, *An American Tragedy*, based on murder of Grace Brown.

1921   "Phantom Gold" (1927)

1923   Publishes *The Color of a Great City* (sketches). Boni & Liveright republish *The "Genius,"* unexpurgated.

"Marriage—for One" (1927)

1924   "Fulfilment" (1927)
"The 'Mercy' of God" (as "The Mercy of God") (1927)
"The Shadow" (as "Jealousy: Nine Women Out of Ten") (1927)

1925   Burton Rascoe publishes first book-length study, *Theodore Dreiser*. Completes, publishes *An American Tragedy*, with immense success.

"Convention" (1927)
"St. Columba and the River" (as "Glory Be! McGlathery") (1927)

1926   Travels to Europe with Helen Richardson. Publishes *Moods, Cadenced and Declaimed* (poems). *An American Tragedy* adapted successfully for Broadway stage.

1927   Publishes *Chains* (short stories). Travels to Russia,

	November-January, upon invitation of Soviets; plans book based upon tour.

"Khat"

"The Price Who Was a Thief"

"Typhoon" (also as "The Wages of Sin")

"The Victor" (also as "Victory")

1928 Publishes *Dreiser Looks at Russia.*

1929 Publishes *A Gallery of Women* (sketches). Stockmarket crash inaugurates Great Depression.

1930 Publishes *Fine Furniture* (long story) with Random House. Studies need for revolutionary economic directions in America and other capitalistic nations.

1931 Publishes *Tragic America* (nonfiction); *Dawn* (autobiography).

1932 Votes Communist ticket in national election. Begins co-editorship of *The American Spectator.* Upon bankruptcy of Liveright transfers to Simon and Schuster. Intensive, but unsuccessful, effort to complete Part III, *A Trilogy of Desire,* under title *The Stoic.*

1932-40 Extensive involvement in public speaking; works on behalf of labor, radical, anti-war movements. Dorothy Dudley publishes major study, *Forgotten Frontiers: Dreiser and the Land of the Free.* Settles in Hollywood with Helen Richardson.

1941 Publishes *America is Worth Saving* (nonfiction).

1942 Sara White Dreiser dies, October.

1944 Travels to New York; accepts Award of Merit medal from American Academy of Arts and Letters. Marries Helen Richardson. Determines to complete long-unfinished novel of Quaker life, *The Bulwark.*

1945 Completes *The Bulwark.* Intensive effort to complete Part III, *A Trilogy of Desire.* Finishes greater part of *The Stoic.* Dies in Hollywood, December 28.

1946 Doubleday publishes *The Bulwark.*

1947 Doubleday publishes *The Stoic.* Howard Fast edits *The Best Short Stories of Theodore Dreiser.*

PLOTS

An American Tragedy, 1925.

I. Clyde Griffiths is the eldest son of an itinerant missionary, Asa Griffiths, and his wife Elvira. When Clyde is twelve, his parents operate the Door of Hope Mission in a poor district of Kansas City. All of the children, Clyde as well as his older sister, "Esta," and the younger children, Julia and Frank, are involved in street preaching, a practice they neither understand nor care for. Before long Esta runs away with an actor who passes through the city with a traveling show.

By the time he is fifteen, Clyde is working full time. First he has a job in a soda fountain and then as a bellboy in the largest downtown hotel in Kansas City, the Green-Davidson. The life of the hotel, a new universe to him, teaches Clyde much concerning money and morality in the modern world, and it instills in him an ambition someday to be rich and lead the same uninhibited life led by many of the hotel guests. The heretofore sexually inexperienced boy becomes infatuated with an incipient prostitute, Hortense Briggs, and soon he is spending a good share of his modest wages in attempting to satisfy her every whim.

Esta Griffiths, pregnant, is abandoned by her lover. Having nowhere to turn, she comes back in disgrace to Kansas City. Mrs. Griffiths proves to be considerably more compassionate than her rather rigidly righteous husband; she undertakes to find Esta a room in which to live while waiting for her child to be born. Clyde accidentally discovers this arrangement, is shaken by his sister's plight, but like his parents is more concerned for the shame her condition brings upon the family. In particular he is worried for fear he may be asked to part with his savings in order to help support Esta.

Clyde joins a group of bellboys from the hotel when they take their girl friends on an automobile ride in a vehicle borrowed illicitly by Oscar Hegglund and driven by his friend Willard Sparser, son of the chauffeur employed by the owner of the automobile. Following an afternoon of driving, drinking, and dancing, the young

men and women head back to Kansas City, speeding en route in
order to make up for lost time. By accident a pedestrian, a young
girl, is struck by the car. But rather than stop for the policeman
who signals them, the group race away. The driver manages to
elude their pursuers, but he crashes the car into a lumber pile and
it is wrecked. Most of the passengers are injured, but Clyde is
unscathed; and concerned only for the potential consequences to
himself should he be discovered, he runs from the scene.

II. Clyde leaves Kansas City hidden in a railroad boxcar. Eventually he reaches Chicago, where he finds work as a bellboy at the
Union League Club. The arrival of a guest at the club, Samuel
Griffiths of Lycurgus, New York, stirs Clyde's memory. This can
only be his uncle, his father's brother, a success in the shirt and
collar business. Introducing himself, Clyde is told that he may
come to Lycurgus if he wishes and work in the Griffiths factory.
He chooses to accept the opportunity, and he travels to upstate
New York, where he finds the Griffiths family supremely well
situated in their small city. Five of them inhabit the palatial home
on Wykeagy Avenue: besides Mr. and Mrs. Griffiths, there are two
girls, Myra and Bella, and a son, Gilbert, who greatly resembles
Clyde in appearance. Rich and privileged, this family exists in a
world far beyond Clyde's fondest dream.

As promised, Clyde is put to work in the factory, first in the
shrinking room. He locates in a commonplace room at Mrs.
Cuppy's rooming house, and for companionship he has his fellow
workers, most of whom he feels are beneath him intellectually
and socially. He is keenly aware of the potential that lies in his
blood relationship to the owner of the factory, and he is overjoyed
when his aunt invites him to dinner at the Griffiths home. While
there Clyde meets another guest of the family, Sondra Finchley,
daughter of a local vacuum-cleaner manufacturer. Beautiful and
impeccably garbed, Sondra comes to epitomize for Clyde the desirable daughters of wealth; but the girl pays him little attention,
and he understands that in a practical sense any aspiration on his
part to such an heiress is probably without foundation.

Before long, Clyde having proved himself at work, he is put in
charge of the stamping room. Here he supervises a group of girls
who mark collars with names and sizes before they go to the stitch-
ing room. His salary is increased from fifteen to twenty-five dollars
a week, and he feels on his way toward a type of success. Among

the girls in his department is one who particularly attracts his eye, Roberta Alden, a farmer's daughter. In spite of regulations discouraging supervisors from fraternizing with their workers, Clyde begins to court Roberta. Soon the two have fallen in love, and Clyde attempts to persuade Roberta into a full sexual relationship. Her home training and her instinct both tell Roberta that she should insist first upon marriage, but eventually the persistent Clyde has his way. The girl casts her entire lot with him, for he is a man she looks up to fully as much as he looks up to Samuel Griffiths; on Clyde's part, unfortunately, affection is limited chiefly to sexual pleasure. His true hopes lie elsewhere.

At this same time, unexpectedly, Clyde encounters Sondra Finchley again. Now she takes an interest in him, first showering him with attention in order to inflame his cousin Gilbert with jealousy and later becoming genuinely fond of him. For Clyde, Sondra represents beauty, money, status, luxury, power: all the desirable and heretofore unobtainable objects of his dreams. Step by step, Clyde is taken into the social circle dominated by Sondra, the Griffiths, and their wealthy friends. He begins to feel accepted as one of them. The notion that he, a poor boy, might aspire to marriage with a girl such as Sondra no longer seems such a ridiculous fantasy. Perhaps, after all, she is within his grasp.

While he continues his affair with Roberta Alden, Clyde deserts her whenever an opportunity arises for seeing Sondra. During the winter social season he becomes increasingly a regular member of the younger set. But now Roberta brings him the alarming news that she is pregnant. Previously she hinted at marriage; now she demands it. Clyde cannot allow himself to consider marriage at such a time as this. As an alternative, he attempts to locate a drug which will cause Roberta to miscarry. That attempt failing, he takes her to a Gloversville physician, Dr. Glenn, where, under the pseudonym of Mrs. Ruth Howard, she requests an abortion. Dr. Glenn refuses on ethical and legal grounds, and he advises her instead to confide in her parents. Roberta is aware by this time that Clyde leads a double life, and she becomes increasingly insistent upon marriage.

Summer arrives in upstate New York. The social leaders of Lycurgus reopen their lodges in the lake district of the Adirondack mountains. Sondra Finchley goes to Twelfth Lake, where she writes to invite Clyde up for a visit. Roberta meanwhile has gone to her parents' home near Biltz, and she also writes Clyde; for he has promised to marry her, and she wishes to know precisely when he will be coming for her. Clyde senses himself caught in a desperate dilemma. He chances to read an Albany newspaper which contains the story of an accidental double drowning. A plan born of desperation occurs to him. He sees Roberta now merely as an obstacle that must be removed from his upward path; since she refuses to remove herself, it is up to him to see that his way to wealth is cleared. It seems an easy thing to duplicate the drowning accident described in the newspaper. Thereby he might rid himself of Roberta and the baby while simultaneously making it possible for him to marry Sondra instead.

Clyde informs Roberta that they will take a honeymoon trip, in the course of which they will be married. Happily she meets him and they go by train to Utica, from there northward to Grass Lake and then on to an even more isolated spot, Gun Lodge on Big Bittern, where Clyde registers as Mr. and Mrs. Clifford Golden. In a rowboat some five hundred feet from shore near the deepest and most secluded section of the lake, Clyde is beset by his driving need to drown Roberta. Simultaneously he is held back from the deed by an opposing sensation, a true revulsion from violence. Roberta notes his strange behavior. She rises in the boat, approaches him, reaches her hand out to him. Clyde reacts automatically, flinging out his hand to keep her from touching him. The camera he carries strikes her in the face, and Clyde rises to assist her and to apologize for the unintended blow. But the shift in their positions rocks the boat. Roberta plunges into the water, her head striking the left wale of the boat as she falls. She screams for help, then sinks. Rather than save her, Clyde, in a dazed state, strikes out for shore, changes his clothes for those in a suitcase he has brought along, buries the wet garments, and heads south on foot for Twelfth Lake and Sondra.

III. All too soon the body of Roberta Alden is recovered from Big Bittern's waters and taken into the nearest town for autopsy. It seems clear to the investigating sheriff and to the medical men who examine the corpse that a murder has been perpetrated. But Clyde has proved a most inept criminal. In his wake he has left clue upon clue. At Gun Lodge, Roberta's possessions yield an unmailed letter addressed to her parents. They are contacted and suggest Clyde as her companion. In his room in Lycurgus are found the agonized letters Roberta wrote him. Much faster than he might have imagined even in his considerable state of apprehension, Clyde is located and placed under arrest for Roberta's murder.

At once the rich world of Clyde's imagining fades. Sondra, her parents fearful of scandal, is spirited far from the possible taint of the trial. The press is persuaded never to mention her by name. Samuel Griffiths furnishes money for Clyde's defense; but, feeling the boy to be guilty and his own association with him to be an unprofitable one, he holds aid to a minimum. In a lengthy trial, Clyde looks on and listens, bewildered, while an untold volume of evidence and an extensive parade of witnesses construct an airtight case for the prosecution. He is easily convicted of murder in the first degree.

With no one else to turn to, Clyde wires his mother at her present mission in Denver. She arrives, is reconciled with her condemned son, and leads the fight to save him from the death penalty. But her efforts, including a final, personal appeal to the Governor, are in vain. Clyde—still bewildered, never certain whether he killed Roberta in cold blood or merely by neglecting to rescue her from the lake—goes to the electric chair.

Agnes Alden, Emily Alden, Ephraim Alden, Roberta Alden, Thomas Alden, Titus Alden, Mrs. Titus Alden, Amanda, Patricia Anthony, Appleman, Legare Atterbury, Maida Axelrod, Harley Baggott, Baker (Clyde Griffiths), Thomas Barrett, Barnes, Dr. Bavo, Roger Beane, Everett Beeker, Alvin Belknap, Dr. Beemis, Dr. Betts, Jack Bogart, Martha Bordaloue, Mrs. Braley, Flora Brandt, T. R. Briggen, Hortense Briggs, "Shorty" Bristol, Darrah Brookhart, Brookshaw, "Bud" Bruning, Burton Burleigh, Catchuman, Dr. Crane, Cranston, Bertine Cranston, Grant Cranston, Mrs. Cuppy, Pasquale Cutrone, Quincy B. Dale, Rita Dickerman, Walter Dillard, Simeon Dodge, Larry Donahue, Mrs. Rutger Donahue, Eddie Doyle, Jack Evans, Opal Feliss, Robert Fessler, Sondra Finchley, Rufus Forster, Joseph Frazer, Reverend Gault, Mrs. Gault, Bert Gettler, Mrs. Gilpin, Stella Gilpin, Dr. Glenn, Clifford Golden (Clyde Griffiths), Mrs. Clifford Golden (Roberta Alden), Carl Graham (Clyde Griffiths), Mrs. Carl Graham (Roberta Alden), Gabriel Gregg, Asa Griffiths, Mrs. Asa (Elvira) Griffiths, Bella Griffiths, Clyde Griffiths, Frank Griffiths, Gilbert Griffiths, Hester "Esta" Griffiths, Julia

Griffiths, Myra Griffiths, Russell Griffiths, Samuel Grif-
fiths, Mrs. Samuel Griffiths, Hadley, Frank Harriet, Oscar
Hegglund, Fred Heit, Paul Higby, Wash Higgins, Mrs.
Ruth Howard (Roberta Alden), Hubbard, Reverend Peter
Isreals, Reuben Jephson, Robert Kain, Kittie Keane,
Ira Kellogg, Kemerer, Jerry K. Kernocian, Arthur Kinsella,
Klinkle, Tina Kogel, Nicholas Kraut, John Lambert, Lig-
gett, Dr. Lincoln, Foster Lund, Lutz, Reverend Duncan
McMillan, Manigault, Grace Marr, Rufus Martin, Orville
W. Mason, Greta Miller, Dr. Mitchell, Thomas Mowrer,
Earl Newcomb, George Newton, Mrs. George (Mary)
Newton, Lucille Nicholas, Miller Nicholson, Scott Nichol-
son, Ruza Nikoforitch, Frederick Oberwaltzer, Edna
Patterson, Hoda Petkanas, Blanche Pettingill, Mrs. Pey-
ton, Angelina Pitti, John Pole, "Polish Mary," Oliver Pope,
Joe Rainer, Louise Ratterer, Mrs. Ratterer, Thomas
Ratterer, Riordan, Isadore Rubenstein, Zillah Saunders,
Frank W. Schaefer, Lena "Dutch Lena" Schlict, Miss
Schoof, Secor, Frederick "Freddie" Sells, Paul Shiel, Sim
Shoop, Orrin Short, Amos Showalter, Zella Shuman, Fred
Shurlock, Albert Sieberling, Laura Sipe, Sissel, Sheriff
Slack, Rudolph Smillie, Willard Sparser, Dr. Sprull, Francis
X. Squires, Arabella Stark, Vanda Steele, Bill Swartz, Ed
Swenk, "Dutch" Swighort, Dr. A. K. Sword, Sam Tacksun,
Burchard Taylor, Violet Taylor, Nina Temple, Harry Tenel
(Clyde Griffiths), Floyd Thurston, Miss Todd, Doris Trine,
Charles Trone, John W. Troescher, Mrs. Truesdale, Doug-
las Trumbull, Gertrude Trumbull, Jill Trumbull, Tracy
Trumbull, Samuel Upham, Wallace Upham, Wallace
Vanderhoff, Governor Waltham, Dr. Webster, Joshua
Whiggam, Whipple, Grover Wilson, Mrs. Grover Wilson,
C. B. Wilcox, Ethel Wilcox, Constance Wynant, Samuel
Yearsley.

The Bulwark, 1946.

Rufus and Hannah Barnes, Quakers, live on a small farm near
Segookit, Maine, happy in the ease with which their remote location aids them and their two children, Solon and Cynthia, in
leading the simple existence prescribed by their faith. When the
boy Solon is ten years old, his uncle, Anthony Kimber, dies in
Trenton, New Jersey, leaving a pottery business to his widow.

She persuades Solon's father to move to Trenton and to manage the sizable estate for her. The real property includes a farm of sixty acres as well as a house which is really a mansion, called Thornbrough, located at Dukla, twenty-five miles from Philadelphia.

Their move completed, the Barnes family live at Thornbrough. Rufus Barnes is a capable woodworker, and he sets about to refurbish the dilapidated mansion, a process which is not completed for many years. The result is ironical, for the nearer Rufus comes to completing his task on the house, the closer he approaches the life of ease and luxury forbidden to Quakers. Nevertheless, Rufus and Hannah make a mighty effort to raise their children in the plain style. For guidance they rely always upon the Inner Light, and they achieve considerable success.

At the Dukla school young Solon meets Benecia, daughter of Justus Wallin, a clever and prosperous Quaker who, besides his Dukla estate, possesses a fine home on Girard Avenue in Philadelphia. He also hold a one-third interest in the city's Traders and Builders Bank. The Barnes and Wallin families become fast friends. Rufus and Solon are taken into Justus Wallin's employ, opening a branch of his business in Dukla, where they offer insurance, loans, and real estate. Solon does well enough at this so that Justus offers to take him into his Philadelphia bank and teach him the banking business from the ground up. This offer pleases Solon, particularly since he and Benecia have grown to love one another. Benecia is only seventeen, too young to hope to gain her parents' consent to a marriage, but Solon's new position makes it possible for them to see each other more frequently.

While Solon makes steady progress at the Traders and Builders Bank, he continues to court Benecia. Within two years Justus Wallin gives his consent. Solon and Benecia are married in the Friends' meeting house in Dukla, afterward returning to Dukla to settle in the home Justus has given them as a wedding gift. The industrious Solon is up at six o'clock every morning to oversee the small farm belonging to the house, after which he takes the train into Philadelphia for his day at the bank. He and Benecia prosper, and yet they determine to conform to the Friends' code of simplicity, keeping their home cleared of all pictures, musical instruments, and newspapers. No books beyond those congenial to Quakerism enter their doors. As the years pass, the Barnes children are born: Isobel, Orville, Dorothea, Stewart, and finally Etta.

Solon's diligence makes the accumulation of wealth inevitable, and yet he is adamant in resisting the use of his money for frivolity. On all sides he is appalled to see examples of Quakers who have fallen to the blandishments of the crassly materialistic life which late nineteenth-century America seems to exalt. In following popular trends, many Quakers have left their Quaker principles behind them in the chase after luxury. Solon's sole aim in life is to preserve himself and his family from slipping away from their faith.

Throughout the region surrounding Dukla, a heavily Quaker area, the Barneses are considered to be ideal examples of communal respectability. But Solon finds it considerably more difficult than he has imagined to order life for his children as conveniently as he has ordered it for himself. His eldest child, Isobel, is not physically attractive, a fact which causes her considerable unhappiness, particularly when her sister Dorothea grows into a genuine beauty. As for Dorothea, she is tempted easily toward beautiful trinkets and a life of ease. The older boy, Orville, is ambitious only for a lucrative business career; he cares little for his Quaker principles except as they may prove to be advantageous to him in that career.

By the time he is forty Solon has risen to the position of acting treasurer in the bank at a salary of $10,000 a year. He is given shares in the bank and placed on the board of directors. His family, coming into greater contact with the non-Quaker world as they mature, are increasingly hard put to continue in the ways Solon has set out for them. Etta attends a boarding school in Chadd's Ford, where she meets Volida La Porte, a Wisconsin girl of considerably diluted Quakerism who influences her to stray from the plain life. Etta's hope is to join Volida in attending the University of Wisconsin, far from her parents' restrictive covenants and watchful eyes.

The younger son, Stewart, also is attracted to things other than Quakerism. His first serious lapse occurs when he violates the proscription against theater attendance by conniving with a group of schoolmates to attend a burlesque show in Trenton. Solon, discovering this, is more seriously disturbed at realizing that Stewart has lied to him; he asks his son never again to tell him an untruth. Stewart promises never to lie, but he has no con-

fidence that he will be able to keep that promise. Solon's path
as a father is not made any smoother when his wealthy relative,
Rhoda Wallin, deliberately encourages Dorothea to follow her own
drift into secular ways. Orville already has drifted that direction.
His ambition in life is to marry an heiress, and he does so.

Etta pleads with her parents for permission to join Volida La
Porte at the University of Wisconsin. She is refused and subsequently runs away from home. In order to join her friend in Madison, she steals two pieces of her mother's jewelry and pawns
them. Solon follows his daughter to Wisconsin, confronts her on
the campus, and pleads for her return to Quaker ways. Etta proves
to be immovable. She cannot see any evil inherent in the secular
studies conducted at Madison, and she refuses to return to
Pennsylvania. While she readily confesses her theft and even
exhibits true remorse at having violated her parents' property, she
is determined to live her own life.

Volida and Etta travel to New York City when the summer term of
school in Madison is over. They take up residence in Greenwich
Village, where Etta becomes a model for a painter, Willard Kane.
Soon she becomes his mistress as well. Orville Barnes chances
to discover this relationship, and he berates Etta for the shame
her affair will bring to the family if it becomes known at home.
Etta in turn accuses Orville of caring for nothing at all but surface
reputation, an accusation which appears to be substantiated
when Dorothea Barnes marries the son of a wealthy street-rail-
way magnate and refuses to invite Etta to the wedding for fear
that the scandal of her immoral conduct in New York would cast
a pall on the festivities.

Stewart Barnes grows into a handsome young man and is sent
to Franklin Hall School. Here his tendency to adopt his com-
panions' way of life intensifies. Without intending harm, Rhoda
Wallin supplies him with money that makes it possible for him to
initiate weekend excursions of which he knows his father would
severely disapprove. On one occasion, telling his parents that he
is going to stay the weekend at Rhoda Wallin's home, he instead
joins two friends, Victor Bruge and Lester Jennings, Jr. The three
take an automobile to Wilmington, Delaware, pick up three girls
and seduce them. In order to finance such escapades, Stewart
begins to filch money from his home, stealing from Orville's
wallet and from Benecia Barnes' purse.

Solon in the meanwhile has discovered that a group of his fellow directors at the Traders and Builders Bank have been using their positions as a cover for lending large sums of money to companies in which they have themselves heavily invested. These loans have been extended on the basis of extremely dubious collateral. Debating this question with himself, Solon is motivated to act upon his conscience. He visits the Treasury Department in Washington, D.C., and alerts government agents to the need for investigating the bank. He understands that his action may mean a scandal will be discovered; he also knows that he may be honor bound to resign his own position as Director.

Stewart goes on another weekend spree with his two schoolmates. This time Victor Bruge has brought with him a medicine filched from his home, a tranquilizing drug which his mother keeps on hand for quieting her nerves. He intends to put a few drops secretly into a drink for his girl friend, Psyche Tanzer, and thereby make her more receptive to his sexual advances. Unfortunately for all of the group, the drug produces unconsciousness in Psyche. The medicine is an opiate, ordinarily harmless, but Psyche has a heart weakness of which the boys are unaware, and the drug works destructively on that. While the group drift aimlessly in their car, terrified at their predicament, Psyche dies, and they are so panic-stricken that they leave her body beside a country road. Soon traced, the boys are arrested. The story makes sensational headlines. Engulfed by shame, unable to face the prospect of seeing his father in his disgrace, Stewart commits suicide in his jail cell.

In the aftermath of this tragedy, Solon informs his board of directors of his part in the government investigation of the bank, and he resigns his position there. Etta's love affair with Willard Kane runs its course and ends, leaving her desolate. She does not return to Pennsylvania for Stewart's funeral, believing that the disgrace she has brought to her parents herself need not be added to their tragedy. But when Benecia suffers a stroke not long after Stewart's suicide, Etta comes back and is reconciled. Ten days afterward, Benecia dies. Solon is dazed by the many blows he has received. For a time his mind is disoriented, and he stands in danger of losing the faith that has been his most precious resource.

Time, rest, and in particular the loving care of Etta work to repair Solon's mind. On the road to recovery, he is stricken with cancer and declines steadily. In three months he is dead. He is buried by his children according to the brief, plain services prescribed for Friends. At his funeral Etta weeps disconsolately. Reproved by her brother Orville, who believes that she—in his eyes the initial cause of all their family woes—is crying selfishly, she assures him that she is not crying for herself at all, nor for her dead father, but for life.

David Arnold, Abel C. Averard, Freeborn K. Baker, Cynthia Barnes, Dorothea Barnes, Etta Barnes, Hannah Barnes, Isobel Barnes, Rufus Barnes, Solon Barnes, Mrs. Solon (Benecia Wallin) Barnes, Stewart Barnes, Compton Benigrace, Jr., Tommy Briggam, Letitia Briggs, Walter Briscoe, Victor Bruge, Alys Burt, Cadrigan, Beryl Cadrigan, Coggleshall, Joseph Coombs, Sutro Court, Sophia Crowell, Luther Dabe, Ethel de Fremmery, Eberling, Judge Ellison, Mrs. Leah Etheridge, Miss Frazer, Alfred Gadge, Pet Gair, Georgette Gilman, Walter Hokutt, Lester Jennings, Jr., Joseph, Willard Kane, Adlar Kelles, Iris Keane, Ambassador Keene, Mrs. Keene, Anthony Kimber, Laura Kimber, Phoebe Kimber, Rhoda Kimber, Ranse Kingsbury, Miss Lansing, La Porte, Volida La Porte, Barnabas Little, Martin Mason, Ada Maurer, Edward Miller, Edward Nearjohn, Ira Parker, Jordan Parrish, Kirkland Parris, Mrs. Kirkland Parris, Percy Parsons, Rae Patterson, Myrtle Peoples, Rita Poole, Prang, Dorothy Prendergast, Adelaide Prentice, Ned Raine, Olive Ritter, Cosmo Rodeheaver, Adlar Sableworth, Susan Scattergood, Georgina Scott, S. Guy Seay, Ezra Skidmore, Althea Stoddard, Edward Stoddard, Isaac Stoddard, Oliver Stone, Psyche Tanzer, Myra Temple, Mrs. Tenet, Regina Tenet, Tomlinson, Ethel Van Ranst, Benecia Wallin (Barnes), Benjamin Wallin, Cornelia Wallin, Hester Wallin, Justus Wallin, Segar Wallin, Jr., Mrs. Segar Wallin, Jr., Marsha Warrington, Mrs. Whittridge, Wilton B. Wilkerson, William "Willie" Woods.

"Butcher Rogaum's Door," 1901. See "Old Rogaum and His Theresa."

"Chains," 1919.
The wealthy Upham Brainerd Garrison, returning home by train from a business trip, stops en route to notify his wife by telegram of the hour of his arrival in the city. During his journey he reminisces, attempting to understand even a little of the import of himself and his life. To himself Garrison is a great mystery.

At age twenty-four Garrison had married Jessica Ballogh, nineteen; but she, discovering almost at once that she had made a great
mistake, left him and obtained a divorce.   Years later Garrison
chanced to be present when the lovely Idelle was carried into
Insull General Hospital following a near-fatal automobile accident.
He visited her often during her convalescence and fell in love with
her. So thorough was Garrison's infatuation that his discovery
that Idelle was by no means the innocent child she appeared to be
could not affect his feelings toward her. Of even less importance to
him was the fact of his own age, forty-eight, which made him more
than twenty years Idelle's senior.

Once married to Idelle, Garrison to his surprise found her to be
sex incarnate. Although young in years, she had already left behind her a considerable trail of wrecked romances, ended affairs,
and broken hearts.   For her sake men had ruined themselves.
Some had attempted suicide. Of greater consequence to Garrison, it became clear that Idelle would not, and in truth could
not, change her ways. She was fully as much the creature of her
sensual nature as she was master of it. But curiously this aspect
of their lives together, painful as it often was for Garrison, served
only to make Idelle the more fascinating in his eyes.

Today, on his journey home to Idelle, Garrison determines that
there must be a major change in her ways. His brief separation
from her has allowed him to achieve a helpful perspective on their
marriage. He has concluded that Idelle as she now exists, openly
and incorrigibly promiscuous, is a menace to him which must not
be tolerated any longer. Love has become a torture for him, albeit
an often-pleasant one. He plans upon his return either to force a
satisfactory agreement with Idelle or to leave her, painful as that
break might prove to be.

When he arrives at his grand home on Sicard Avenue, Garrison
is disappointed to find that Idelle is away. A note has been left
behind for him. He becomes infuriated when he realizes how
little importance his wife has attached to his homecoming. His
first, emotional impulse is to file at once for divorce. He begins to
pack a valise so that he may leave the house and never return.
Later, somewhat more calm, he opens Idelle's note. Its affectionate tone causes a weakening of his resolve. Idelle disclaims any
responsibility for being away from home rather than remaining to
greet him. His telegram came too late, she says, for her to change
her plans, and she begs him to join her in attending the house
party being given by her friend Betty Gildas. She has gone on to

the Gildases' ahead of him; he must come as soon as he arrives in the city.

When Garrison chances to look at their wedding photograph standing on his bureau—Idelle at a lovely twenty-four—he is seduced all over again. Rather than finish with the packing of his suitcase, he orders his car brought around and directs his chauffeur to drive him to the Gildases' to join his wife. Garrison realizes that his life is as mysterious as ever; he remains an uncomprehending, helpless creature of love, which can be the most punishing and inscrutable of human emotions.

Arbuthnot, Jessica Ballogh, Gaither Browne, Dr. Dorsey, J. Coulstone, Upham Brainerd Garrison, Mrs. Upham Brainerd (Idelle) Garrison, George, Betty Gildas, Gatchard Keene.

"Convention," 1925.

A staff artist working for a Midwestern newspaper relates his experiences with his friend Wallace Steele, a reporter on the same paper. Both men have been assigned to create a Sunday feature dealing with the steamboats which ply the local stretch of river, carrying principally young lovers on holiday excursions.

Steele's wife being absent from the city, he brings his landlady, Mrs. Marie Davis, as a companion on the cruise. Mrs. Davis turns out to be a very pretty girl in her mid-twenties. His action raises some quite natural questions about Steele in the artist's mind. Then, in the process of making his sketches aboard the steamship, he finds that one affectionate couple whom he discovers in the shadows and uses as a model is in actuality Wallace Steele and his pretty friend. The portrait which he has sketched, when sufficiently disguised, appears as an illustration in the Sunday feature story for which it was intended.

Sometime later the artist has an opportunity to meet Steele's wife for the first time. Mrs. Steele turns out to be a rather plain and faded woman. Because she appears to be so altogether unsuited to the reporter's personality, she causes the artist to ponder the deep errors into which human beings are lured by love. Two months after this encounter, Mrs. Steele is taken dangerously ill. The cause is said to be a box of poisoned candy, delivered through the mail. The victim, when she has recovered sufficiently to speak, accuses Marie Davis of attempting to murder her.

To the staff artist, who is assigned to sketch her for the news-

paper, Mrs. Davis declares her innocence. She and Wallace Steele
have been lovers; this she admits proudly. It is true also that Mrs.
Steele has refused to grant her husband a divorce. But Mrs. Davis
dispels the notion that she feels any need for a marriage ceremony
in order to bind her love. For this reason she denies having any
real motivation for attempting to poison Mrs. Steele.

Steele himself, somewhat more thoroughly a creature of convention, fears the adverse publicity which is certain to stem from
the attempt on his wife's life. When questioned, he vehemently
denies that his affection for Mrs. Davis runs as deeply as she has
suggested. The newspapers understandably make much of the
emotional aspects of this love triangle, and in his official investigation the District Attorney concludes that it was Mrs. Steele herself who purchased the box of candy bearing the poison. When
Mrs. Steele confesses to the deed, Marie Davis is released from
police custody. No charge is made against Mrs. Steele; it is
decided that she has suffered sufficiently. The unpredictable
public, emotionally affected by her attempt at a blood sacrifice in
the name of love, is swayed heavily to her support. She becomes
temporarily a heroine to the local "sob sisters" of the press.

A group of reporters question Wallace Steele as to his future
intentions. He replies that he will of course remain with his wife.
He describes Marie Davis as being no better than a prostitute, and
he swears that he is through forever with women such as she. The
reporters, however, rather than being edified by Steele's gra-
tuitous rejection of his mistress, are offended. They consider him
to be little more than an abject slave to popular conventions. As a
result, his reputation suffers badly, and he is never rehired on the
staff of any local newspaper.

When the staff artist chances to encounter Wallace Steele and
his family in New York some years subsequent to this episode,
the artist is struck once again by the thought that the husband
and wife are a total mismatch. Their predicament seems to him
a cold and sad, but not uncommon, miscarriage of human love.

Mrs. Marie Davis, Wallace Steele, Mrs. Wallace Steele.

"The Cruise of the 'Idlewild,'" 1909.

A group of workers in a planing mill attempt to circumvent the
dull routine of their day. A suggestion is made that they recreate
the mill in their imaginations, making it into a ship, themselves
acting as its crew. Because the mill is located at seaside, on

Long's Point, where the Harlem River meets the Hudson, the suggestion is not wholly implausible, and it is accepted.

The unnamed narrator, a worker in the engine room, suggests
that the men call their "craft" the "Idlewild." It is a name he con-
ceives of as a jest: the workers will furnish the "idle," their bosses
the "wild." The idea of a ship takes hold. Old John, the engineer,
becomes Captain and the narrator his first mate. The Smith is
appointed bos'n, and Little Ike, his helper, is made bos'n's mate.
The engine room is turned into the Captain's cabin. In the men's
daily conversation, sailors' jargon becomes the order of the day.

For a time all goes well, and one after another of the mill workers
is brought in to augment the "crew" of the "Idlewild." The game
furnishes them all with a new interest in life. But after a while the
men manifest a tendency to play practical jokes on the bos'n's
mate, Little Ike, and he resents this. Eventually their tendency to
make him the butt of their humor backfires. Ike complains to the
shop foreman (who is not eligible to participate in the "Idlewild"
game) that his floor is being strewn two and three times daily with
wood shavings which he is obliged to sweep up. In the interest of
efficiency, the foreman calls a halt to this practical joking.

This marks the beginning of the end for the "Idlewild"; Ike's
action constitutes "mutiny," and the Captain and mate have no
way of dealing with it. Next, the Captain and the mate themselves
fall out over a matter of priority, with the inevitable result that in
company with their failure to maintain official status, the ship
itself "goes down." In time the "Idlewild" becomes no more than a
nostalgic memory.

At one point, in later days, it is suggested that perhaps the craft
might be "raised" and be known by a new name, "Harmony"; but
when Little Ike hears of this plan, he threatens openly to quit his
job rather than see another situation arise in which he might be
plagued as he was before. The notion of resurrecting the "Idlewild" is dropped. The men return to their ever more monotonous
daily routine.

Stephen Bowers, Cullen, Ike, Joe, "Old John."

The Financier, 1912.

In 1837 a son is born to Philadelphia banker Henry Worthington
Cowperwood and his wife. The boy, named Frank Algernon, is
mentally alert and physically handsome. As he grows he proves
to be a natural leader and a fearless fighter, instinctively prag-

matic, and fascinated by economic and political life. His world view is established early when, still a boy, he observes an aquarium tank in which a squid is devoured by a lobster. The lesson is simple and direct: if life must feed on life, better to be an armed lobster than a defenseless squid. Frank Cowperwood understands that his natural talent is for business and finance, directions in life which are encouraged at home by his father's dinner-table talk of complex deals and fat profits. Frank is alert also to the honor accorded his uncle Seneca Davis, a self-made plantation owner from Cuba.

Frank Cowperwood's first independent business deal occurs at age thirteen when he bids at auction for seven cases of soap, then arranges to dispose of it to his neighborhood grocer at a profit of about a hundred percent. At age fourteen, Frank already wants to leave school to engage the practical world full time, and only a word of caution from his uncle Seneca dissuades him from it. However, at seventeen, without waiting to complete his final year of high school, he goes to work for the grain-and-commission house of Henry Waterman and Company. There he proves his talents almost at once, learns rapidly the principles which govern success in the brokerage business, and at Christmas time is rewarded with a $500 bonus. Until this time Frank has been serving without pay as an apprentice; now the Watermans offer him a weekly wage of twenty dollars. But Frank soon leaves them for a better post with Tighe and Company.

Through his parents Frank Cowperwood meets Alfred Semple and his wife Lillian. At nineteen Frank has known many girls; but Lillian Semple, even though she is twenty-four, catches his eye. Judging principally from appearance—she is attractive without being flashy—he considers her to be the type of wife a rising young businessman such as himself ought to have. Tighe and Company put young Cowperwood to serve on the floor of the stock exchange under their floor man and manager, Arthur Rivers, as one of a number of operators who buy and sell on small orders. In this capacity Frank learns the mechanisms of the stock market as rapidly as he learned the grain commission business while at Waterman's.

When Cowperwood is twenty, Alfred Semple dies of an unexpected illness. At about the same time Cowperwood's uncle, Seneca Davis, dies also and leaves him a bequest of some $15,000. With this money Cowperwood is enabled to go into

business for himself. Soon he is courting the widow Semple, and
before long they are married. In time two children arrive, Frank,
Jr., and then Lillian. With a growing family and his own business,
Cowperwood prospers on all sides. He aspires even higher, of
course, even to the wealth and power of the great established
financiers: Drexel & Co., Jay Cooke & Co., Gould & Fisk. The Civil
War arrives, and with it comes the need for immense loans to
finance the campaigns. These generally are entrusted only to the
largest and soundest financial companies; but Cowperwood, in
aggressive pursuit of his interests, obtains the chance to place a
fraction of one of the war loans—a million dollars—as a means of
establishing his reputation in Philadelphia.

One of the men whom Frank Cowperwood approaches in selling
his war loan is a wealthy Irishman, Edward Malia Butler, a self-
made man who started life as an illiterate slop collector. Now
Butler, blessed with excellent political contacts established over
the years, owns a huge contracting firm with an extensive business
in city water mains and sewers. Cowperwood has come to Butler's
attention through their mutual interest in the streetcar companies
just then being organized as a new mode of urban transportation.
While conferring with Butler, Cowperwood is introduced to the
man's seventeen-year-old daughter, Aileen, a lively, high-spirited
beauty who catches his eye at once and causes him to reflect
somewhat ruefully upon the fact that Lillian has appeared to fade
in beauty since the day he married her. He determines that he
will purchase property on Girard Avenue near the Butlers and
build a new home, the more adequately to express his new wealth;
he persuades his father to buy an adjoining plot and build a home
for himself next door.

Frank Cowperwood's success in placing his war loan marks him
as potentially a financier of note and a man to be reckoned with
in Philadelphia. By chance, his dealings with Edward Butler have
put him into intimate contact with one of the three major political powers in the city, the other two being Henry A. Mollenhauer
and Senator Mark Simpson. Through Butler he makes the acquaintance of George W. Stener, newly elected as City Treasurer. Stener
has a proposition to offer. Cowperwood will be given $200,000 in
city loans with which to speculate, his mission being to bring them
up to par value on the local market. With the money received, the
city will pay off outstanding warrants long overdue. A certain
amount of manipulation is needed in order to create sufficient de-

mand to bring the newer loans up to par; but Cowperwood, having
the entire issue at his disposal, can withhold or release enough at
a time to control the supply. He and Stener stand to profit mightily.

For Cowperwood the advantage is double. He gains the power
to raise or to lower the market price of the loan certificates almost
at will. And because he has an effective monopoly upon the total
loan, his credit rating with the local banks rises astronomically.
Both for himself and for George Stener he begins also to speculate
heavily in streetcar companies, using money which Stener ap-
propriates temporarily and on a quasi-legal basis from the city
treasury. Cowperwood reasons that so long as he and Stener work
hand in glove and the "loans" invariably are returned intact to the
treasury for audit, little risk is run. He begins to dream of a city-
wide streetcar monopoly owned perhaps by himself. Henry
Worthington Cowperwood, in part due to his son's spectacular
rise, becomes President of the Third National Bank.

On Girard Avenue the two Cowperwood homes rise as symbols
of postbellum affluence. Frank Cowperwood begins to collect
paintings, statuary, and other *objets d'art*. A grand reception is
planned for the opening of the two homes. The Butler family is
invited; and Aileen, now a headstrong nineteen and drawn
irresistibly by Cowperwood's magnetic force, sees the ball as an
opportunity for becoming more intimately acquainted with him.
She dresses brilliantly for the occasion, aims to attract Frank
Cowperwood's eye, and succeeds. Within three months the two
are lovers, and Frank leases a house on North Tenth Street where
they can meet in private.

For six years, until he is thirty-four, Frank Cowperwood deals with
George Stener, and both become rich. Frank has spread himself
thin with expenses and obligations, but since he has guarded his
public reputation zealously he sees no reason why he should not
continue to prosper, almost automatically. Then, in October 1871,
the great Chicago fire occurs, causing a financial panic whose
shock waves extend to Philadelphia and beyond. Cowperwood
finds himself temporarily overextended and unprepared to meet
calls on his loans or to remit cash withdrawals made by clients of
his brokerage house. He has invested a half million for Stener,
counting on having the money returned with a profit as his city-
loan certificates rise in value, but instead the panic drives prices
downward. The streetcar-company stocks he has given to the
city's large banks as collateral on loans plunge also; at their lower

prices they will be insufficient. Time is what Cowperwood needs, and time is what he does not have. Lacking outside help, he is in real danger of having his loans called and thereby being forced into bankruptcy.

Frank Cowperwood's logical source of aid is his friend Edward Butler, to whom he appeals, in the process necessarily revealing to Butler the questionable activities he and Stener have been engaging in. Before Butler can provide aid, he receives an anonymous letter exposing Cowperwood's seduction of his daughter. Aileen denies the accusation, but her father is certain she is lying to him. His reaction is to call at once the loan he has given Cowperwood previously: $100,000. At the same time, George Stener, panicky at fear of being discovered as an embezzler, demands that Cowperwood replace the half million dollars belonging to the city treasury. And Cowperwood, faced with the realization that every man in finance is now placing his own interests above all others, is unable to borrow sufficiently to cover his obligations. His brokerage house is forced to suspend. Within days, this failure is followed by public exposure of the Cowperwood-Stener misuse of municipal funds. Both men are indicted for embezzlement.

Frank Cowperwood has risen quickly, but he has fallen even more rapidly. His business life is ruined, and his family life has deteriorated badly. His wife also has received an anonymous report of her husband's philandering. Cowperwood establishes a new rendezvous in which to meet Aileen, she being now the single ray of cheer in his life; but Edward Butler discovers this new love nest and visits it to confront Cowperwood and Aileen directly. Told that she will be sent away from Philadelphia until she has recovered from her infatuation, the defiant Aileen leaves home secretly and hides in the home of her dressmaker, Mrs. Calligan, whose daughter Mamie was her schoolmate. This act of defiance only increases her father's determination to see Cowperwood jailed.

At his jury trial Cowperwood is convicted, along with George Stener. He appeals his case, and the appeal fails. He is sentenced to four years and six months in the Eastern Penitentiary of Philadelphia. In prison he is a model prisoner. He rejects the temptation to become despondent at his condition. Instead, he reflects deeply upon the path by which he has come to this prison cell. It is not that he has done wrong that disturbs him, but that he has been careless, has let his guard down long enough to be caught by circumstances. He vows never to allow this to happen again. If ever he is able to rise again—and he is confident that he will—he determines to be altogether ruthless and self-serving, the only way, as he sees it, by which he can assure his survival in a cutthroat world.

To prepare for the day of his release from prison, Cowperwood asks Lillian to give him a divorce so that he can cast his lot with Aileen. She refuses, but Edward Butler's death removes the other major obstacle to his plan for marrying Aileen. After thirteen months in prison, Cowperwood is pardoned through the efforts of financiers and politicians who think it not beneficial to their own interests that one of their number should remain jailed as a convicted felon. Ever alert to the future, Cowperwood before going to prison has employed an underling, Stephen Wingate, to handle his business and personal affairs while he is incarcerated. Wingate also has been guided in establishing a dummy corporation through which Cowperwood, the true controller of the house, might re-enter financial life without incurring the prejudice which will necessarily work against an ex-convict.

Having planned so well, Cowperwood is ideally prepared for the panic which follows the failure of Jay Cooke & Co. in September 1873. Business follows business into overnight bankruptcy; the stock market plummets. In order to fuel the panic, Cowperwood instructs Wingate to dump all his holdings at prices far below even the depressed levels then existent; and as his ruse succeeds, triggering a precipitous decline of confidence and subsequently of prices, Cowperwood comes back into the market with a vengeance. While others are unloading their properties at any price offered, he is buying steadily and at consistently reduced values. Within days he has made more than a million dollars. He is richer than he ever was before.

Cowperwood's new opportunity has arrived. He is thirty-six, free, and full of plans. When Lillian is persuaded to give him a divorce, his last problem appears to be solved. However, given his embezzlement conviction and his divorce, it is not convenient for him to remain any longer in Philadelphia; so after reconnoitering potential sites for relocation Cowperwood settles upon Chicago as the ideal spot for an entrepreneur of his stamp. With Aileen at his side, he sets out for that city and a new life.

Charles Ackerman, Thomas Alderson, Ammerman, Patience Barlow, Judge Beckwith, Julian Bode, Walter Bonhag, Jacob Borchardt, J. J. Bridges, Aileen Butler, Callum Butler, Edward Malia Butler, Mrs. Edward Malia Butler, Norah Butler, Owen Butler, Katharine Calligan, Mamie Calligan, Elias Chapin, Tom Collins, Patrick Gavin Comiskey, Sister Constantia, Jay Cooke, Anna Adelaide Cowperwood, Edward Cowperwood, Frank Algernon Cowperwood, Mrs. Frank Algernon (Lillian Semple) Cowperwood, Frank Algernon Cowperwood, Jr., Henry Worthington Cowperwood, Mrs. Henry Worthington (Nancy Arabella Davis) Cowperwood, Joseph Cowperwood, Lillian Cowperwood, Dalrymple, Adam Davi, Father David, Mrs. Davis, Seneca Davis, Mrs. Seneca Davis, W. C. Davison, Michael Desmas, Francis Drexel, Wilton Ellsworth, William Eugster, Doris Fitler, Benjamin Fraser, Fletcher Gray, Genderman, Red Gilligan, Simon Glassberg, Francis J. Grund, Jacob Harmon, Harry Hibbs, Charles Hillegan, Albert Hursted, Adlai Jaspers, Frewen Kasson, Kathleen Kelly, Thomas Kelley, Roger Kendall, Judge Kitchen, Kugel, Walter Leigh, Philip Lukash, "Spat" McGlathery, Manuel, Richard Marsh, Gilbert Martinson, Judge Marvin, Alta Mollenhauer, Caroline Mollenhauer, Felicia Mollenhauer, Henry A. Mollenhauer, Mrs. Henry A. Mollenhauer, Montague (Frank A. Cowperwood), Mrs. Montague (Aileen Butler), Philip Moultrie, Fletcher Norton, August Nunnekamp, Marcus Oldshaw, Judge Wilbur Payderson, Richard Pethick, David Pettie, Andrew Pohlhemus, Able Protus, Judge Rafalsky, Judge Rainey, Terrence Relihan, Arthur Rivers, Emily Rivers, Sampson, Scanlon (Edward Malia Butler), Alfred Semple, Mrs. Alfred (Lillian Wiggin) Semple, Sister Sempronia, Abner Sengstack, Dennis Shannon, Senator Mark Simpson, "Wash" Sims, Judge Smithson, Bailiff Sparkheaver, Marjorie Stafford, Stapley, Steemberger, Harper Steger, Steinmetz, Mrs. Steinmetz, George W. Stener, Albert Stires, Avery Stone, Gordon Strake, Edward Strobik, Newton Targool, Washington B. Thomas, Edward Tighe, Joseph Tisdale, Guy Tripp, Frederick Van Nostrand, George Waterman, Henry Waterman, Sr., Henry Waterman, Jr., Richard Webber, Skelton C. Wheat, Hosea Whitney, David Wiggin, Stephen Wingate, Winpenny, William Woodruff, Robert Wotherspoon, Thomas Wycroft, "Eddie" Zanders, Joseph Zimmerman.

Fine Furniture, 1930.

Opal, a waitress with grandiose notions, marries Clem Broderson, a husky and rough-hewn logger. Opal persuades Clem to spend his savings of $3000 on elegant furniture through which she hopes to transform the tiny, plain house supplied to them in the logging camp at Red Ledge. Her furniture is wholly out of place. It identifies her as a social rival of Mrs. Saxstrom, wife of the Red Ledge camp superintendent. It also becomes a point of contention with Clem's associates, who see through Opal's pretensions and are angered when she makes it clear that they are not welcome in her house wearing their logging clothes. In time Clem loses his friends on this account, and because Opal refuses to accept any but the most desirable location for a home in the new camp being established by the logging firm, he loses his job also. Belatedly, Clem understands the truth, that his wife and her fine furniture have brought him nothing but ruin.

Martin Binwool, Mrs. Martin Binwool, Clem Broderson, Mrs. Clem (Opal) Broderson, Ella Citron, Jig Citron, Mrs. Jig Citron, Goole, George Parch, Bud Rokes, Olaf Saxstrom, Mrs. Olaf Saxstrom, Mark Stark, Mrs. Mark Stark, Orville Wilkins.

"Free," 1918.

At dawn in his Central Park West apartment, architect Rufus Haymaker contemplates the terminal illness of his wife, Ernestine. At age sixty, Haymaker realizes that his thirty-one years of marriage have not been happy, largely because he and his wife are a mismatch. The two were childhood sweethearts, but even prior to their wedding Haymaker knew that marriage would be a mistake. Foolishly, as he now understands, he bowed to convention and married Ernestine regardless, never letting her know that his passion had long since cooled.

Rufus Haymaker thinks of himself now as resembling the legendary Spartan boy who kept the raging fox hidden beneath his cloak and never let on that the animal had gnawed away his vitals. He came to realize only gradually what a total creature of convention he had married; Ernestine proved to be utterly incapable of understanding his—the artist's—point of view. Love, he concludes, is truly blind. Children were born to him and Ernestine, bringing with them a temporary and somewhat deceptive sense of contentment. But the children are long grown now, married, and gone from home. It seems to Haymaker that Nature, if it did anything, conspired for its own dark purposes to entrap him into the married state.

It strikes him as true that Nature cares nothing for individual wishes or happiness, but is concerned always and only with propagation. His children appear to be passing through marital traumas not altogether unlike his own. He thinks of his friend, Zingara, a man who has achieved true greatness as an architect. Zingara has avoided marriage entirely; Haymaker ponders the possibility that, for one who wishes to do great things, Zingara's may be the ideal, perhaps the only route.

Haymaker is beset by all these thoughts late into the night; he finds his mood fluctuating wildly. First he is torn by his honest desire to be free of Ernestine. Next he is overcome with emotion at thoughts of the long and ineradicable ties he has established with his wife over the years. As Ernestine's condition worsens, and then, as she dies, he realizes also that his potential for achievement is gone now, vanished; it has seeped away year by year. He is free now, yes; but at this late stage of life his freedom is no more than the freedom to die.

Fred Barlow, George De Gaud, Mrs. George De Gaud, Irma De Gaud, Mrs. Elfridge, Miss Filson, Ethelberta Haymaker (Kelso), Rufus Haymaker, Mrs. Rufus (Ernestine) Haymaker, Wesley Haymaker, Horner Kelso, Mrs. Horner (Grace) Kelso, John Kelso, Mrs. John (Ethelberta Haymaker) Kelso, Dr. Storm, Mercedes Westervelt, Zingara.

"Fulfilment," 1924.

In the boudoir of her mansion the wealthy Ulrica begins her day. She ponders the imminent return of her husband, Harry, from a western journey. She married Harry in a moment of weakness following the unexpected death of her lover, Vivian, a painter. To Ulrica, although Harry was just fifty, he seemed an old man. But he was rich and insistent, and she gave in to his persuasion.

While she has her breakfast and orders her chauffeured automobile to be brought around, Ulrica reflects on some of the men in her crowded past. There was the young and rather indifferent Byram when she was only seventeen; he was the first. Then there was Newton, a successful businessman; then Joyce, a real-estate plunger, long on material comforts but short on spirituality, art, or any true sense of romance, elements on which Ulrica thrives. Then came Edward, to be followed by Young, and afterward by Karel, rich and socially prominent. After him, Loring, the physician.

During the morning, while she shops for jade pins and has her ermine cape revamped, Ulrica continues her reminiscing, thinking now particularly of the happy arrival in her life of the Rocky Mountain sheep-rancher's son, the dark-eyed, sallow-skinned Vivian—at last her dream come true. But Vivian was bone-poor, and so was she. No one would pay money for the canvases Vivian painted, although now, thanks to Harry's help in popularizing him, his work went for ten and twelve thousand a picture. Life works in strange ways indeed.

And then Ulrica's success in the theater arrived, a small triumph, true, yet sufficiently remunerative to underwrite her life with Vivian, to begin helping him by purchasing necessities for his studio. And then the great blow at her existence, Vivian's sudden death in the influenza epidemic. She herself had been half dead and unable fully to comprehend her loss. Her bowl of joy was dashed from her fingers even as she sipped from it. If only Harry were not coming back into her life, she speculates. She wishes he would stay away and leave her in the bittersweet world of memory. She determines to break off with him.

Ulrica has come to a position in life in which she possesses both money and friendship in good measure. Yet, without Vivian, all seems to turn to ashes. Life seems to her to be truly perverse: first it sweats and agonizes one, then showers one with luxury. She reminds herself of Harry, who also rose from poor beginnings, a man who at fifty found that his millions were worthless to him without someone to share with. And so Harry found her, and she him. They are so much alike, she admits, the two of them.

And still, their similarities aside, Ulrica knows that she can never love Harry. While she ruminates the mystery of existence, he arrives home. Despite her resolve not to see him, Ulrica orders the maid to send Harry up to her room and to lay out her green evening dress for the social activities she knows he will have planned for them tonight. Life goes on, and one must go with it.

Harry, Ulrica, Vivian.

The "Genius," 1915.

I. Eugene Witla is the son of a sewing-machine agent. He grows up in Alexandria, Illinois, during the 1880s. His parents, Thomas Jefferson and Miriam Witla, also have two daughters, Sylvia and Myrtle, both somewhat older than Eugene. The boy's principal character trait is an intense affinity for beauty which makes it predictable that he may one day become an artist. This trait manifests itself also, as he matures, in a strong sex urge; Eugene develops a fixation upon lovely teen-aged girls which never diminishes.

At age seventeen Eugene acquires his first genuine girl friend when Stella Appleton, his own age, moves from Moline, Illinois, enters the local high school, and becomes acquainted with Myrtle Witla. At the close of his second year of high school, Eugene obtains a job setting type for the *Morning Appeal*, a newspaper which is run by Benjamin Burgess, father of Sylvia Witla's prospective husband. Here the boy comes to know and to like Caleb Williams, the editor of the paper, Jonas Lyle, the head of the composing room, and John Summers, a handyman. By virtue of this employment also, Eugene comes to know and to like newspaper work.

As Eugene grows to manhood and feels the urge to be independent, editor Caleb Williams advises him to go to Chicago. His innate skill at drawing makes it likely that he will find employment in the city as a newspaper artist, illustrating stories and advertisements. Eugene at first is indecisive; but because Stella Appleton resists his sexual overtures and eventually, because of his insistence, breaks off with him, he determines to take Williams' advice. He leaves at once for Chicago, hoping to earn as much as seven or eight dollars a week and thereby support himself. Traveling to the city by train, Eugene is tremendously impressed by the growing city's great structures, its crowds of people and clatter of traffic. After ten days, however, he still has not located a job with a newspaper. His funds run low; he takes work at a hardware store repairing second-hand stoves, loses that post after two weeks, and then becomes a runner for a real-estate concern, with a route which introduces him to fine areas such as Michigan and Prairie Avenues.

When this job ceases with the failure of the real-estate concern, Eugene works as driver for a laundry. He meets Margaret Duff and is initiated sexually. His next employment is as a collector for The People's Furniture Company. His wages of fourteen dollars a week are sufficient so that he can save enough money to pay his tuition at the Chicago Art Institute, where he enrolls for evening courses. His mind now is on a career in the art field. He is inspired by a painting of a nude by the acclaimed French artist Bouguereau then on exhibit in Chicago, and when he at last takes his place in a class, drawing from a nude model, he feels that he is headed toward his true vocation.

At this time Eugene is nearing the age of twenty. Because he has been in Chicago for over two years without returning home, he goes to Alexandria to visit his parents. While there he is introduced to a beautiful visitor, Angela Blue, a Wisconsin girl some five years his senior. Eugene finds her beauty irresistible. Her blue eyes and yellow hair combine with a perfect figure to make her an ideal. Conversing with Angela, Eugene learns that she is a schoolteacher. Their conversation reveals also that their basic differences in life philosophy and their codes of behavior are great. Yet they are mutually attracted. They take the same train back to Chicago and before parting promise to write each other. Eugene progresses satisfactorily with his courses at the Art Institute. In need of a companion for a student dinner, he invites a classmate, Ruby Kenny, to accompany him. These two soon find themselves involved in a passionate affair. This relationship continues, regardless of Eugene's strong feelings for Angela Blue, sentiments reinforced during Angela's periodic visits to her aunt's home in Chicago. Still something of an idealist, Eugene reasons that his connection with Angela is pre-eminently a spiritual one, whereas that with Ruby Kenny is wholly physical. Without his being fully aware of it, this attitude comes to characterize his thinking about Angela.

Five months after his first meeting with Angela, Eugene proposes marriage, and she accepts. Following his first term at the Art Institute, Eugene secures a position with a newspaper; here he makes drawings for reproduction, discovers that he can write as well as draw, and soon is busy producing illustrated essays on local topics. As he progresses, the newspaper's friendly Sunday Editor advises him to think of trying his hand in New York. The Eastern metropolis holds infinitely greater opportunities for a man with Eugene's talents, particularly in the magazine-publishing field.

Eugene travels to New York, and the huge city both exhilarates and frightens him. He finds lodgings on West 14th Street and attempts to break into the world of magazine illustration, but he finds the field already dominated by established artists whose talents equal his own or surpass them. He manages to obtain small assignments sufficient to support himself, after which he initiates a series of paintings in which he hopes to capture the raw beauty of New York's streets and its amazingly diverse population. He produces a number of these paintings. One nighttime scene of working girls flooding into the streets after a long day in the factories is sold to *Truth*, a weekly magazine, for $75.00. Eugene becomes friendly with Hudson Dula, the magazine's art director. Dula purchases a number of the young artist's drawings. Eugene feels that he is on his way. He is happier than he has ever been, and so fully occupied that a year and a half pass before he thinks seriously of Angela Blue and his promise to her.

Eugene returns to Angela's hometown, Blackwood, Wisconsin. He attempts to seduce his fiancée, without success, and while one side of him is pleased at her reluctance to yield, another side questions whether her rigid conventionality is well matched with his increasingly liberal notions of sexual freedom. It is disturbing also for him to find that Angela's sister Marietta, his own age, twenty-two, is fully as attractive to him—and perhaps more so—as is she. He returns to New York, where he meets Miriam Finch, a sculptress ten years his senior. She is beautiful as well as distinguished; they become lovers. Some months after this, he meets Christina Channing, a singer, and finds himself strongly attracted to her sexually. At the same time, he feels bound by strong and disturbing emotional ties to Angela Blue. Both Miriam and Christina contribute substantially to Eugene's education in the arts, and during the next summer, rather than visit Angela, Eugene vacations at Christina's cottage, Florizel, in the Blue Ridge Mountains. Having read Herbert Spencer's philosophical book *First Principles* and other such modern, scientifically oriented volumes, he has concluded that human life is without solid basis or coherent meaning; one's happiness must be snatched whenever and wherever it can be. Christina's philosophy is remarkably similar to Eugene's; she yields herself to him with no thought of obligating him, preferring a career over marriage.

Although Eugene has been engaged to Angela for three years, he has not seen her now in eighteen months. She writes to say that she is ready to be married; her sister Marietta also writes, telling Eugene of Angela's unhappiness over the possibility that he may no longer care for her. He returns to Blackwood, where the disconsolate and somewhat desperate Angela gives herself to him in return for an assurance of marriage.

II. Eugene is fully aware that his passion for Angela Blue has cooled; yet he marries her out of a sense of duty, and they settle in the Washington Square section of New York. Angela is intimidated by the greater sophistication of Eugene's many lady friends in the arts. The fact that Eugene has kept their marriage a secret leads her to suspect that he is ashamed of her, and she reproves him for it.

Eugene enters his painting "Six O'clock" in a competition held by the American Academy of Design. Not only is it accepted for hanging, but some critics pronounce it the best canvas in the exhibition. This measure of success inspires him with hope of obtaining a one-man show. He approaches M. Charles, manager of the prestigious Kellner and Son gallery, who is so taken with Eugene's paintings that he grants him a show free of charge. The critics' reactions to this event are mixed; some find Eugene's urban subject matter shabby, unattractive, and non-artistic, while others hail him as a new master of modern "fresh-from-the-soil" realism. The sale of three paintings for a total of $1,300.00 marks the show as a success, and on these proceeds Eugene and Angela travel to Paris, where Eugene paints a series of pictures for a new exhibition, returning to New York in the autumn.

Before his new show can open, however, Eugene is afflicted by a disabling neurasthenia which he attributes to sexual overindulgence. He fears his talent is seeping away, and his spirits sink when his new show is less enthusiastically received than was his first. He determines to leave New York and move to Chicago, hoping to be able to work better there. In packing for their move, Angela comes upon a box of love letters from Ruby and Christina, and her resultant emotional tantrum brings Eugene even closer to an emotional collapse. He is deeply depressed, convinced that his marriage has been a deranging mistake; he fears that he is going insane. For a time the couple move in with Eugene's parents, but while they are in Alexandria Eugene meets and falls in love with Frieda Roth, the beautiful eighteen-year-old daughter of a neighbor. Discovering this, Angela is moved to new recriminations.

Eugene is puzzled at his seeming inability to avoid being attracted to other women. He is convinced that some biological necessity beyond either his understanding or his control is involved. He and Angela initiate a period of wandering. They live for a time in Chicago, then in Kentucky, then on the Gulf Coast, while he tries to paint, unsuccessfully. In desperation he returns to New York, sending Angela to stay with her parents until he might be able to call for her. When he is unable to obtain employment elsewhere, he manages to find work as a day laborer on the railroad, stationed in the carpenter shop at Speonk, just outside the city. He finds the work hard but therapeutic. In Speonk Eugene rents a room from Mrs. Hibberdell. Before long her daughter, Carlotta Wilson, comes to visit. A beauty, she revives Eugene's flagging sexuality, reciprocates his passion for her, and for a number of weeks joins him in a romantic affair. One day Mrs. Hibberdell discovers them and removes Eugene from the premises by announcing a temporary closing of her boarding house.

Carlotta returns to New York. Angela, separated from him for seven months, arrives in Speonk to live with Eugene. He well understands that society would label Angela a good woman, Carlotta a bad one, and that according to society's code he ought really to prefer Angela. Nevertheless he much prefers Carlotta. More accurately, he wishes he might possess them both. Before long Angela becomes aware of his duplicity and accuses him of having betrayed her; meanwhile, beset by antagonistic forces, his romance with Carlotta has ebbed.

As he recovers from his neurasthenia, Eugene returns to Manhattan and obtains employment illustrating the daily headlines as a newspaper artist on the staff of the *World*. Success here brings him a considerably better position as Art Director with the Summerfield Advertising Agency. His salary rises consistently. He rents an apartment for Angela on Central Park West; and, at least on the surface, their differences appear to have been repaired. Success breeds success. The Kalvin Publishing Company of Philadelphia offers Eugene a position at an $8,000.00 beginning salary, and he accepts. The next year his salary is raised to $10,000 and the year following to $12,000 annually. Angela, determined to preserve her marriage and convinced that one day she may need to play upon Eugene's sense of obligation in order to do so, considers having a child by him. She consults a physician who examines her and assures her that despite her age she should, given proper treatment, have no problem in conceiving.

In New York Hiram C. Colfax of the giant United Magazines Corporation, hearing of Eugene's abilities, offers him $18,000 a year to become Advertising Manager, an offer Eugene cannot refuse, particularly when an eventual salary of $25,000 as Art and Editorial Manager is suggested. He and Angela move back to New York, rent a sumptuous apartment on Riverside Drive, and when the

UMC moves into its skyscraper offices, Eugene feels that he has achieved the pinnacle of success. Angela is not quite so fortunate, as Hiram Colfax doubts her ability to fit congenially into the clever, artistic, moneyed crowd at UMC, a doubt shared by Eugene, who begins to neglect her again. Kenyon C. Winfield, a real-estate plunger whom Eugene has known since his days with Summerfield, persuades Eugene to invest heavily in the construction of a new suburb to be promoted by his Sea Island Development Company in the area beyond Gravesend Bay.

III. Through Hiram Colfax Eugene meets Mrs. Emily Dale, a young widow of Staten Island, who becomes his friend and Angela's. At a reception he meets Suzanne, Mrs. Dale's beautiful daughter, with whom he falls into an instant infatuation. He finds it possible to pursue this acquaintance at a number of social gatherings; then Angela is stricken with a rheumatic fever attack, and Suzanne comes to the apartment on a regular basis to read aloud to her. Touched by his apparent devotion to his ill wife, Mrs. Dale invites Eugene to spend a recuperative weekend at their country place. Thus she inadvertently provides him with an occasion to take a further step toward his planned intimacy with Suzanne. Before long, head over heels in love, he is declaring himself openly to her.

At UMC Eugene's success has engendered a formidable rival in Florence White, some years his elder and envious of him since his first days at UMC. White has worked tirelessly to denigrate Eugene in the eyes of Hiram Colfax; and as Eugene comes to concentrate his thoughts increasingly on Suzanne Dale, he plays into White's hands by neglecting his responsibilities sufficiently to provide his rival with an opening for criticism. Eugene is unconcerned, for at this moment Suzanne has shown signs of reciprocating his love; the two search out more opportunities to be together, always running the risk of being found out by Mrs. Dale and by Angela, of course.

Eugene has come to resent Angela bitterly by now and sees her as the major obstacle blocking his desire to possess Suzanne. Eventually, at a reception held at the Witlas, Angela comes upon her husband with the girl in his arms. Rather than berating him, Angela attacks Suzanne, challenging her expectation that anything other than misery can ever come of this romance, seeing that Eugene will never be granted a divorce. Suzanne learns from Angela that she is merely the most recent in a considerable chain of mistresses, all of whom have had their moment and passed. To cap the situation, Angela announces that she is at long last pregnant with the child she has counted on to bind Eugene to her in a permanent fashion. Eugene wishes to believe that Angela is lying about the pregnancy; but when he learns that she is not, he is more miserable than ever, feeling that she has deliberately connived to entrap him.

When Angela suggests that she will inform Mrs. Dale of the romance, Eugene swears that he will leave her if she breathes a word of it. However, provided she remains silent, he will stay with her, reserving only his freedom to see his lover whenever he desires. This ploy works well enough until Mrs. Dale, unaware of her daughter's involvement, suggests that she and Suzanne spend the fall and winter months abroad. Suzanne is thrown off her guard, and only partially aware of what she is doing, protests that she must remain near the man she loves: Eugene Witla. Her mother is aghast at learning the truth. She visits Angela in order to learn more of the details of the affair; then she confronts Eugene in his office. Unless he will agree to end the affair, he will be exposed to his employer, Hiram Colfax.

In order to preserve Suzanne from the inevitable consequences of public exposure, Mrs. Dale contrives with her son, Kinroy, to spirit her daughter away to Canada. Eugene pursues them, forcing Suzanne's return to the United States. At UMC Eugene's neglect of his position has accelerated criticism of his stewardship and allowed his rivals to weaken his base with Colfax. The supposition at the office, where his involvement with Suzanne is unknown at this time, is that his involvement with the foundering Sea Island company has distracted him from his editorial responsibilities. Then Mrs. Dale, forced to the wall by Eugene's intransigence, informs Colfax of the facts regarding his seduction of Suzanne. Colfax offers Eugene a clear choice: he can avoid a scandal by renouncing the girl, or he can resign his post at UMC. Mrs. Dale succeeds in persuading Suzanne to test her love by waiting a year before going to Eugene. If after that time she still wishes to join her lover, she may do so with her mother's blessing. Suzanne accepts this plan. Eugene realizes that it means there is a good likelihood Suzanne may be lost to him forever.

Because he will not renounce Suzanne, Eugene loses his job with the United Magazines Corporation. He breaks the lease on his expensive apartment and takes separate rooms, leaving Angela. His sister Myrtle attempts to rescue him from the despondency which sets in. She hopes to persuade him to accept her own new-

found panacea, Christian Science, a faith which he finds most
irritating in its particulars even though it seems to correlate generally with his own notion that large areas of life are illusory. He
goes so far as to visit a practitioner, Mrs. Althea Johns, in the
unrealized hope of finding solace. Eugene is separated from
Angela; yet he feels tied to her strongly by obligation, particularly
since her health is endangered by her weak heart. Her final months
of pregnancy are spent in a maternity hospital. Her condition
deteriorates, and at the last moment a Caesarian operation is per-
formed in the hope of saving both mother and child. But Angela
dies in spite of all that medicine can do. Eugene is widowed, left
with his daughter, whom he names Angela, to care for. At the
behest of his former gallery manager, M. Charles, he returns to his
painting, a stronger artist than before. Some years after all of this
is over, Eugene and Suzanne Dale chance to meet on Fifth Avenue
in New York, and they pass each other without acknowledge-
ment.

Stella Appleton, M. Arquin, Frank Bangs, Mrs. Frank
(Myrtle Witla) Bangs, Baker Bates, Vincent Beers, Oren
Benedict, Jack Bezenah, Angela Blue (Witla), Benjamin
Blue, David Blue, Jotham Blue, Mrs. Jotham Blue, Mariet-
ta Blue, Samuel Blue, Temple Boyle, Benjamin G. Bur-
gess, Henry Burgess, Mrs. Henry (Sylvia Witla) Burgess,
Christina Channing, Anatole Charles, Hiram C. Colfax,
Mrs. Emily Dale, Kinroy Dale, Suzanne Dale, Timothy
Deegan, Malachi Dempsey, Miss De Sale, Mrs. Desenas,
Russell Dexter, Dodson, Margaret Duff, Hudson Dula,
John "Jack" Duncan, Miriam Finch, Harry Fornes, Fred-
ericks, Pottle Frères, Mitchell Goldfarb, Brentwood Had-
ley, William Haverford, Carter Hayes, Mrs. Hibberdell,
Woodruff Hobson, Horace Howe, Jans Jensen, Bill Jef-
fords, Mrs. Althea Johns, Joseph, Obadian Kalvin, Ruby
Kenny, Henry Kingsland, Dr. Lambert, Henry Larue,
Henry C. Litlebrown, Jonas Lyle, McHugh, Marchwood,
Jeremiah Mathews, Joseph Mews, Townsend Miller, Mrs.
Townsend Miller, Henry Mitchly, Adolph Morgenbau,
Owen Overman, John Peters, Herbert Pitcairn, Frieda
Roth, George Roth, Harvey Rutter, Saljerian, Luke Severas,
Philip Shotmeyer, Davis Simpson, Joseph Smith, Jack Stix,
Jimmy Sudds, Daniel Christopher Summerfield, John Sum-
mers, Thompson, Isaac Wertheim, Richard Wheeler, Flor-

ence J. White, Norma Whitmore, Caleb Williams, Mrs.
Norman (Carlotta Hibberdell) Wilson, Kenyon C. Win-
field, Eugene Thompson Witla, Myrtle Witla (Bangs),
Sylvia Witla (Burgess), Thomas Jefferson Witla, Mrs.
Thomas Jefferson (Miriam) Witla, Dr. Willets, Dr. Latson
Wooley, Eberhard Zang.

"Glory Be! McGlathery," 1925. See "St. Columba and the River."

"The Hand," 1919.

Davidson and Mersereau are prospectors in the Klondike at the
turn of the century. After making a rich strike in the gold fields,
they fall out. Davidson believes himself to be the superior businessman, and by virtue of that ability he considers that he is not obli-
gated to share their profits equally with Mersereau.

Aware of his partner's duplicity, Mersereau threatens to retaliate
by exposing certain shady doings from Davidson's past. Davidson
bludgeons him to death. Before he dies, Mersereau raises his right
hand in an attempt to obtain a death clutch on his killer's throat,
but the effort fails. Davidson returns to the two men's home town
in the state of Mississippi. After a rainstorm one day he finds that
water dripping through a leak in his roof has imprinted his ceiling
with a strange and disturbing pattern; it resembles the print of a
giant hand. To Davidson the handprint appears to be a sign that
Mersereau is alive and bent upon vengeance.

Davidson consults with Mr. and Mrs. Pringle, spiritualists, in an
attempt to learn the truth about Mersereau's angry ghost. Following an evening session with these two concerning the phenomena of
table rapping and clairvoyance, Davidson hears a disconcerting
tap, tap, tap on his dressing table. Then the voice of his murdered
partner comes to him, swearing to dog his trail until he dies.

In a dental office Davidson chances to read a magazine article
in which professional spiritualists are presented as being capable
of causing the physical imprints of hands and faces to appear on
glass plates. The photographs which accompany this article look
far too much like the dead Mersereau to be anything else. Before
long, Davidson begins to hear loud, crashing noises near him whenever he goes in public; these seem to draw public attention to him
everywhere. He becomes increasingly upset; his nerves are badly
frayed. When he visualizes a dark cloud, resembling smoke and
materializing into a fist which closes down powerfully upon his

throat, Davidson consults a doctor. The physician dismisses the mystic phenomenon as being plain delusion.

Davidson moves about the continent, attempting to escape from the avenging spirit of Mersereau; but in Battle Creek, Michigan, he hears his victim's voice plainly inform him that henceforth he will be unable to eat. Following this experience, Davidson finds invariably that his food is tainted. He is obliged to live on a diet of fresh fruit and newly baked bread. He can sleep only with a bright light burning, and still the weird, threatening shapes seem to hover in the air around him. He hears Mersereau's voice, threatening, promising to choke him to death.

In his desperation, Davidson commits himself to a private hospital. His throat and stomach complaints are diagnosed officially as symptomatic of an advanced case of tuberculosis. But this medical explanation for his problems does so little to calm the patient that hypnotism has to be considered as a potential remedy. Rather than finding himself helped in the hospital, Davidson experiences a broadening of his delusions to include the medical staff itself. He now imagines that all of the hospital personnel are in league with Mersereau, and thus out to do him in and to cover his murder with their own false diagnosis of tuberculosis of the throat. Soon Davidson dies a horrible death. At the end his own hand is found to have his throat held in a fast grip.

Davidson, Huldah, Miss Koehler, Miss Liggett, Dr. Major, Mersereau, Pringle, Mrs. Pringle, Dr. Scain.

"Jealousy: Nine Women Out of Ten," 1924. See "The Shadow."

Jennie Gerhardt, 1911.

In 1880 Jennie Gerhardt is eighteen years old, a resident of Columbus, Ohio. The illness of her father, an injured glass blower, has put the family under severe economic pressure. Of the six Gerhardt children, only the oldest boy, Sebastian ("Bass"), is of working age, and he earns a mere four dollars a week. In order to make ends meet, Mrs. Gerhardt is reduced to scrubbing floors at the Columbus House, a local hotel. Jennie assists her in these duties.

As a means of generating additional income, Jennie and her mother take in laundry from hotel guests. George Sylvester Brander, a single man of fifty-two and a United States Senator from Ohio, becomes their client. When Jennie delivers his clean laundry one day, Brander questions her about her family. Gradually he becomes interested in the Gerhardts as an instance of the poor but proud American working class. At Christmas time, by chance observing the Gerhardts gleaning coal from where it has fallen beside the railroad tracks, the Senator determines to help the family in any way he can without causing them embarrassment. He visits the Gerhardt home, brings presents for Mrs. Gerhardt, and locates a job for Jennie's father. He admits to himself that he has fallen in love with the sweet-tempered Jennie, and he considers the possibility that he might marry her, send her to a private school for an education befitting a Senator's wife, and then bring her to Washington. On a carriage ride he broaches this subject to Jennie.

Senator Brander's visits to the Gerhardt home, meanwhile, together with Jennie's regular trips to and from the hotel with the Senator's laundry, have not failed to raise comment among both the hotel staff and the Gerhardt neighbors. The gossip reaches William Gerhardt's ears. He, a strait-laced Lutheran with rigid codes of moral behavior, forbids Jennie to see Brander again. But her mother, a more lenient person, aids her to continue seeing the Senator. The father, discovering this, confronts Brander directly. Assurances that the man's intentions are honorable fail wholly to convince Gerhardt, and he asks Brander not to see Jennie again. Soon afterward Bass is arrested while picking coal off a railroad car, and Jennie appeals directly to Brander for the ten dollars required to bail him out of jail. In the emotional aftermath of Bass's release, the Senator makes love to Jennie.

The beginning of the legislative session takes Senator Brander back to Washington, D.C. He promises to send for Jennie so that they might be married. In a stroke of bad luck, the Senator is stricken with typhoid. Jennie's first news of his illness comes by way of the newspaper report which tells that he has unexpectedly died. The heartbroken Jennie discovers that she is pregnant. When her father learns of this he accuses her of having put herself on a level with a common streetwalker. In a display of his inflexible morality he orders her from the home as a contaminant to the rest of the family. Bass aids his sister in renting a room in another part of the city. Mr. Gerhardt, feeling himself irreparably damaged in Columbus by Jennie's disgrace, gives up his work and goes to Youngstown, Ohio, to seek employment. Bass moves to Cleveland, where he is hopeful of finding a better-paying job. If he is successful, he intends moving the family there.

Jennie gives birth to a daughter. When the child is six weeks old
Bass persuades Jennie to join him in Cleveland, where he has
found work to be plentiful. Jennie joins Bass, leaving her baby
girl with her mother. She finds a place as a housemaid with the
Henry Bracebridges on Euclid Avenue. Before long the Gerhardt
family are moved and installed together in a small cottage in Cleveland. At Christmas time William Gerhardt joins them, and he and
Jennie are reconciled to an extent. Jennie's child has never been
baptized. Gerhardt insists upon this being taken care of at once,
and the child is carried to the nearby Lutheran church and there
christened Wilhelmina Vesta.

At the Bracebridge home Jennie is noticed by a visitor, Lester
Kane, son of a wealthy carriage builder of Cincinnati. At age thirty-
six Lester is a pragmatic and experienced man of the world, a
perennial bachelor. He feels drawn irresistibly to Jennie and
wishes to possess her; but he feels that it is unnecessary and even—
considering the variance between their social classes—undesirable
that they marry. Jennie is strongly attracted to Lester and feels
herself succumbing to his magnetic appeal. She has no hope that
he will ever marry her. Indeed, because of her affair with Senator
Brander, she has come to consider herself unmarriageable. At this
juncture William Gerhardt, severely burned on the hands in an
industrial accident, is out of work once again. When Lester Kane
begs Jennie to meet him secretly at a hotel, she does so, largely in
order to importune him for money to help her family. Lester
gives her $250 and extracts from her a promise to come with him
to New York under the guise of accompanying Mrs. Bracebridge
on a trip. Only her mother is taken in Jennie's confidence regarding
this journey.

In New York Lester is convinced that Jennie somehow must be
made his own. Until he can work out some more permanent arrangement, he sends her home to Cleveland. In order to avoid
embarrassment with his own family, he considers the possibility
of settling with Jennie in Chicago, far from the eyes of his parents
and brothers and sisters. He is concerned especially that his
conventional and righteous brother Robert shall never find out
about Jennie and perhaps inform their father, Archibald, who has
long insisted that Lester marry. Jennie introduces Lester to her
father as a boy friend who has come to court her; by degrees she
paves the way for an announcement that he wishes to marry her.
Without telling Lester about the existence of Vesta, she leaves the

child with her mother and goes to Chicago to live with her lover. Her father believes her to be married.

After three years Mrs. Gerhardt dies. Jennie takes Vesta to Chicago and without Lester's knowledge installs her in the care of a Mrs. Olsen. She is able to visit her daughter on a daily basis while Lester is at work. All goes well until Vesta's existence is revealed inadvertently during an emergency illness; Lester, to Jennie's surprise, tells her to bring the child to live with her at the apartment he maintains for her. As time passes he becomes fond of Vesta and she of him, known to her as "Uncle Lester." During an illness Lester stays at Jennie's apartment rather than at the hotel, in order that she might nurse him. During this time his sister Louise visits Chicago and happens upon the two of them together. Outraged at Lester's behavior, Louise returns to Cincinnati and informs the rest of the Kane family of his guilty liaison.

Robert Kane visits Lester in Chicago to urge his brother to abandon Jennie before they become the target of public gossip. His interest is in safeguarding the family pride and in seeing that Lester marries conventionally and well, preferably to some Cincinnati girl of his own Roman Catholic faith. Lester, on the other hand, while refusing to state his long-range intentions regarding Jennie, does make it clear to Robert that he does not expect to abandon her summarily after her years of loyalty to him. On her own part, Jennie is convinced by Louise's reaction to the ménage that society is right in its judgments; she sees herself as a bad woman. In order to put things right, she determines to leave Lester and return to Cleveland, where she will live with her father, now old, alone, unhappy, and in need of her care.

Before she can accomplish this move, Lester discovers her intention. Although presented here with a ready-made chance to be easily rid of Jennie should he wish to do so, he begs her to remain with him. His inducement takes the form of a private house in the Hyde Park area, one with a piece of ground, a home to which Jennie can bring her father to live with her and Vesta. She persuades old Gerhardt to make the move to Chicago only by telling him that she and Lester are married. In Hyde Park the group live very happily together, except for the social isolation which inevitably occurs when the neighborhood comes to understand the true relationship between Lester and Jennie.

Dissatisfaction grows within the Archibald Kane family at the manner in which Lester has chosen to deal with Jennie. Archibald

Kane himself believes that his son should have married Letty
Pace, a local girl who had been romantically interested in Lester
and who meets every social and religious stipulation the family
wishes to apply. Kane calls Lester to Cincinnati for a lengthy,
frank conference after which he advises his son that he has two
choices: he may leave Jennie or he may marry her, but the family
will not tolerate her continuation as his mistress. The father's will
is about to be drawn; it will surely reflect the conditions of this
ultimatum. The story of Lester and Jennie's hidden life reaches
the Chicago newspapers. Their pages openly comment on the
scandalous romance between the lady's maid and the millionaire,
including photographs taken surreptitiously of the couple. By
this time Lester is forty-six and Jennie twenty-nine, and they have
spent their best and happiest years together.

Archibald Kane dies. His will provides well for all of his children;
but as promised, his bequest to Lester is made contingent upon
Lester's actions in regard to Jennie. For three years Lester will be
given the sum of $10,000 annually. If he leaves Jennie, his full
share of the millionaire's estate will be his at once. If he marries
Jennie, he will continue to receive the annual stipend of $10,000,
to him a paltry sum. If he refuses either to leave Jennie or to marry
her, he will, after the three years are up, receive nothing more.
Lester is shocked to think that his father would carry out his
threats in this manner. He is faced now either with abandoning
Jennie or with abandoning his prospects for wealth.

While pondering his decision, Lester takes Jennie with him on a
world cruise. At a number of ports he encounters Letty Pace, his
former Cincinnati girl friend, now the widow of Malcolm Gerald.
Jennie is struck by the thought that these two, Lester and Letty,
belong together by virtue of their similar backgrounds, educations,
interests, and tastes, whereas she herself always feels ill at ease
among Lester's friends. On their return home Lester looks about
for a place in the carriage business, only to find that his brother
Robert has put together a conglomerate corporation which controls
a near-monopoly in carriage construction, thus effectively elimina-
ting any chance that Lester might enter independently into that
business, the only one he knows.

Turning in another direction, Lester invests $50,000, the bulk
of his financial resources, in a real-estate development which goes
sour and is sold at sheriff's auction. Letty Pace Gerald moves to
Chicago and attempts to persuade Lester that for the sake of his

own future and security he must leave Jennie. Old Gerhardt dies, but not without effecting a genuine reconciliation in which he begs Jennie's forgiveness for his obtuse and unnecessarily cruel manner of dealing with her problems in years past. Robert Kane, surmising that since Lester has not already married Jennie he has no intention of doing so in the future, sends an attorney to Chicago to seek her out and apprise her of the conditions of the Archibald Kane will, which Lester has kept secret from her. When she understands that she is a financial liability to Lester, she agrees with the attorney that he must not be allowed to lose his inheritance. He will leave her, or she will leave him, but one way or another they must separate and assure his future; this is her decision. She confronts Lester with her knowledge of his father's will, and by slow degrees it evolves that she will separate from him and move with Vesta to quarters elsewhere.

Lester, having conformed with his father's instructions, takes his place in the family business. Eventually he marries Letty Pace Gerald. Jennie and Vesta live together in their suburban home in Sandwood, near Kenosha. When Vesta is fourteen she is stricken with typhoid and dies, leaving Jennie alone and despondent. Lester returns to Chicago in an attempt to comfort her; he promises to help her in her plan to adopt another child, someone upon whom to lavish her love and affection. He regrets not having married Jennie, he tells her; his own life has changed greatly, but it has not become better or been made any happier. He feels as helpless as a pawn moved over a chessboard by circumstances he neither understands nor controls.

Jennie does adopt a daughter, Rose Perpetua, and they live together in a neighborhood near Jackson Park in Chicago. After a time she adopts a boy, Henry. In all her life Jennie has found happiness only in giving; and giving now, she is happy again. Lester and his wife live in New York, but on a visit to Chicago when he is nearly sixty years of age, Lester takes ill. Letty being in New York and about to embark for Europe, he sends for Jennie. She comes to the Auditorium Hotel and nurses him through what turns out to be his final illness. Before he dies, he tells her quite candidly that they should never have allowed themselves to be parted. To hear these words is all that Jennie can ask.

Made anonymous by a heavy veil, Jennie attends the church services held in Chicago for Lester, and she goes to the railroad depot in order to watch from afar as her lover's coffin is boarded on the train for Cincinnati, where he will be buried in the Kane family plot. Ahead of Jennie lies a life devoted to her two adopted children. She intends to see them raised, started in the world, married perhaps. After that, what may come remains a mystery. Life will go on; that is all she knows.

Mrs. Williston Baker, Bauman, Henry Bracebridge, Mrs. Henry (Minnie) Bracebridge, Senator George Sylvester Brander, Mrs. Craig, Mrs. Davis, Berry Dodge, Dr. Ellwanger, Dr. Emory, Mrs. Hanson Field, Genevieve "Jennie" Gerhardt, George Gerhardt, Martha Gerhardt, Veronica Gerhardt, Sebastian "Bass" Gerhardt, Wilhelmina Vesta Gerhardt, William Gerhardt, Mrs. William Gerhardt, William Gerhardt, Jr., Hammond, Marshall Hopkins, Amy Kane, Archibald Kane, Mrs. Archibald Kane, Imogene Kane, Lester Kane, Mrs. Lester (Letty Pace Gerald) Kane, Louise Kane, Robert Kane, Dr. Makin, Manning, Jefferson Midgely, Miss Murfree, O'Brien, Mrs. Olsen, Samuel E. Ross, Albert Sheridan, Mrs. Sommerville, Mrs. Jacob Stendahl, Henry Stover, J. G. Stover, Mrs. J. G. (Jennie Gerhardt) Stover, Rose Perpetua Stover, Dwight L. Watson, Otto Weaver, Will Whitney, Pastor Wundt.

"Khat," 1927.

In Hodeidah, the Moslem city in the Mugga Valley, Ibn Abdullah, the beggar, contemplates his future. He has come from the village of Sabar in the center of the region where khat, the Arabian stimulant, is harvested. Ibn has become accustomed to his regular ration of the delicious leaves, but now he is unable to afford any khat at all. His craving has increased in the proportion that his purchasing power has diminished. He thinks of ways in which he might obtain a little khat for himself.

A caravan heavily laden with khat leaves comes along. Ibn Abdullah follows the camels as they bear their precious burden to the city's bazaar. There, while others more affluent than he purchase one quantity and another, he is forced to lag behind, penniless, contemplating how he might obtain even a single leaf. He notes a servant buying a large quantity of khat for the splendid wedding feast to be given at the marriage of the daughter of a tin seller. He follows the servant to the place of the wedding, where he begs for alms and is rudely ejected from the premises.

Lacking success among the merchant class, Ibn approaches the coolies and water carriers of Hodeidah. Although they are of a lower caste than he, at least they can afford to eat and to purchase small amounts of fresh khat for their pleasure. But here too Ibn is reviled. Despondent, he walks out into the desert and lies down on the sands, stretching himself out prone, his head pointed in the direction of Mecca. Without khat life seems something not worthy to be endured. He plans to die here in the desert. He will return to Allah as worthless as he came.

Ibn Abdullah, Ahmed, Haifa, Al Hajjaj, Hussein, Bab-al Oman, Waidi.

"The Lost Phoebe," 1916.

For forty-eight years following their marriage, Henry and Phoebe Ann Reifsneider live together happily on the farm which was Henry's boyhood home. Of their seven children, three have died; the others, in true American fashion, have scattered across the continent throughout the Midwest and West. At age sixty-four Phoebe dies; and Henry, despite his children's offers to take him in, chooses to continue living at the home place. He does so, becoming ever more morose and introspective.

In his loneliness Henry comes to believe that Phoebe's ghost visits him, but an imaginary argument drives this spirit away and he is left desolate. Before long Henry alarms his neighbors by making persistent inquiries as to whether they have seen his Phoebe in the vicinity. One neighbor, Matilda Race, concerned that Henry should be wandering the countryside, attempts to detain him at her house; but he insists upon pursuing his quest for Phoebe, whom he now considers to have wandered off and become lost. For a number of years Henry persists in his deranged search for her. He becomes known through all the territory as a pathetic figure.

On a night seven years following Phoebe's death, Henry hallucinates, overwhelmed by the belief that his wife's spirit, returned at last, wishes him to follow her. He obeys the call, trailing this will-o'-the-wisp across the fields until at last he tumbles over Red Cliff and falls a hundred feet to his death. In his way, Henry has found his Phoebe at last.

Dodge, Matilda Race, Henry Reifsneider, Mrs. Henry (Phoebe Ann) Reifsneider.

"Love," 1919. See "Chains."

"McEwen of the Shining Slave Makers," 1901.

Robert McEwen, seated under a birch tree on a burning August day, looks down to see a line of black ants scurrying past his feet. He falls into a reverie. In his dream he becomes an ant himself and is at once involved in the struggle taking place in the ant world between the armies of the black ants and the red ants.

Hidden in the grass, he observes a line of red Sanguineae ants returning from war. They bear with them the corpses of black Fuscan ants they have slain. These ants attack McEwen's new ant friend Ermi, and McEwen comes to the rescue. A savage battle ensues, during which McEwen and Ermi manage to escape underground into the tunnel headquarters of the black ants. McEwen spends considerable time here learning all the curious ways of ants.

The impending war between the Red Slave Maker ants and the Shining (black) Slave Maker ants grows ever nearer. The black (Lucidi) ants raid their neighbors in order to obtain supplies of food sufficient to nourish them throughout the interminable struggle to come. When the Lucidi feel ready they engage the Sanguineae in conflict. McEwen, attacked by four savage red ants, is mortally wounded.

At this juncture McEwen awakens. In the grass at his feet he sees the actual ant battle taking place. He is struck by the inescapable similarity between ant and human ways, and in particular by "this odd, strange thing called *life*" which seems to be represented here in microcosm.

Ermi, Maru, Robert McEwen, Og, Om, Ponan.

"Marriage—for One," 1921.

The clerkly Wray, a friend of the story's narrator, is an average man with an average ambition. His great hope is someday to become a middle-range executive of the great financial concern which employs him and thereby to earn a salary of perhaps six thousand dollars annually.

It is Wray's fond belief that life is just. He proceeds on the assumption that an industrious and honest man will invariably do better than a man lacking those traditional virtues. He believes also that if one takes care in selecting a wife, choosing a woman who has similar qualities and is of the same stature mentally as himself, then the marriage must be a success.

Accordingly, when Wray marries, he uses these principles in making his selection. The girl of his choice is a stenographer who comes from a very strait-laced family, churchgoing to the extreme, anti-theatre in prejudice, and in all other ways ultraconservative. Wray delights in the prospect of his educating Bessie out of her old ways and into new interests which match his own, such as history and philosophy. He undertakes the education of his wife with enthusiasm, and he achieves a success greater than he has bargained for.

Not long after their marriage, Bessie joins a literary society composed chiefly of women whom Wray finds overly aggressive for his taste. It becomes clear to the narrator, if not to Wray himself, that Bessie has been emancipated to a degree beyond what her husband has planned. Trouble is in the offing. Wray intended to be Bessie's mentor; now the tables appear to be turned. As her reading and theatrical interests race beyond his own, Wray finds himself quarreling with her. Before long she has left their apartment, taken a room elsewhere, and resumed her stenographic career. She now considers Wray to be narrow, stubborn, and somewhat beneath her, intellectually. She wishes to end the marriage. All this change has occurred in a space of three or four years.

After some months Wray and Bessie come to an understanding. She returns to him, they take a larger apartment, and she is given a free rein to pursue her new interests. A daughter is born to the couple, but Bessie refuses to become a conventional mother and hires a nursemaid so that her own busy affairs will not be interrupted unduly. When Bessie graduates in her intellectual studies to Freud and Kraft-Ebbing, Wray is genuinely shocked. The narrator is not surprised when he hears that Bessie has left Wray again, taking the daughter, Janet, with her.

A year and a half pass. The narrator now meets Wray once again. The clerk engages him in a lengthy recital of his woes, Bessie's various duplicities, and the total irony of their relationship. Bessie has gone off to California with another man, Wray has heard, and he expects that he will never see her again. He feels certain that his daughter is now lost to him. And still, in the face of his troubles, he continues to love Bessie; he cannot explain why. It is a mystery. To Wray, and to his narrator friend as well, the emotion we choose to call love is a powerful and inscrutable force.

Wray, Mrs. (Bessie) Wray, Janet Wray.

"Married," 1917.

Musician Duer Wilde has been married to Marjorie for only four months when he comes to understand that his marriage has been a tragic error. He has married precisely the wrong kind of girl.

When seen only in her native habitat, the Iowa farm where she grew up, Marjorie displayed a certain infectious charm. But her ideas prove to be too restricted, her attitudes too conventional for the avant-garde studio group with whom Duer associates. Marjorie's theory that one's romantic interests are circumscribed by the one-life, one-love principle contrasts sharply with the theories held by the sexually liberated women with whom Duer works in the New York musical and theatrical world.

Duer holds a reception for a group he considers to contain his more conservative acquaintances, hoping thereby to acclimatize Marjorie more gradually to the new universe of behavior which is New York. The ploy fails. At once it is clear that Marjorie intends that Duer shall relinquish all of his old friends completely. He is the talented one, she argues, and they are mere hangers-on. She protests that Duer cannot afford to let parasites be so free with his talent and his time.

Very little of this side of Marjorie was apparent to Duer before their wedding. But now that she is Mrs. Duer Wilde, Marjorie shows herself openly determined that he shall understand that he is *married*, in the full extent of what that term implies for her. In this new dispensation Duer must avoid any words and actions which Marjorie considers to be vulgar. He must abandon any persons whom she judges to have fallen below her own rigid standards of behavior. For Duer the regimen rapidly becomes intolerable.

Not entirely without justification, Marjorie identifies a number of Duer's women friends as real or potential rivals for his affections. She sets out to eliminate them entirely from his circle. In their place Marjorie favors men who have amassed solid achievements in commerce and finance, however tenuous or even nonexistent their ties with the world of art. The wives of these businessmen prove to be much like Marjorie herself. She feels at ease in their company. With them she can talk freely of cooking, sewing, and housekeeping, whereas when the conversation turns to music, literature, or painting, she is rendered silent and bitter.

When she is obliged to mingle with artists, particularly if they be women, Marjorie develops symptoms of paranoia. She comes to believe that every artistic woman is out to steal her husband. The result is endless quarrels and tears. Duer is torn. He recalls the freshness, the unspoiled emotions that first caused Marjorie to appeal to him. He wonders why these qualities vanished when Marjorie moved to New York.

Duer comes to a clear understanding of his predicament. He realizes fully that, while he is filled with pity for Marjorie, he does not truly love her. She will never change; therefore she can never hope to fit in with the crowd he belongs to. That this should be so represents to him a portion of the unavoidable sadness and tragedy that characterize life.

Mildred Ayres, Georges Bland, Sydney Borg, Francis Hatton, Melville Ogden Morris, Mrs. Melville Ogden Morris, Joseph Newcorn, Mrs. Joseph Newcorn, Charlotte Russell, Ollie Stearns, Duer Wilde, Mrs. Duer (Marjorie) Wilde.

"The Mercy of God," 1924. See "The 'Mercy' of God.

"The 'Mercy' of God," 1924.

The story's narrator holds a philosophy of life which approximates the Hindu indifference to action. His neurologist friend holds the belief that one's direct participation in the strife is the only thing making life endurable. The two discuss a third man, a mechanist. He believes life to be unplanned. It is a cosmic accident, no more, and it is an unavoidable experience.

Now the neurologist expresses a new belief, lately found, which holds that something in nature tends toward a harmonious balance rather than toward a cruel indifference. He provides a concrete example to bolster his suggestion of beneficence in nature. He once knew a family named Ryan, whose two daughters were a study in contrast. Marguerite, the younger, was of a morbid personality, the result of an unfortunate absence of physical beauty which left her with a poor complexion and a disfiguring birthmark above her left eye. But her older sister, Celeste, was the picture of grace and beauty, and her personality was bright and full of color.

As Celeste's popularity grew, Marguerite sank further into a state of withdrawal. She found a safe refuge in reading. Books provided her with a vicarious participation in areas of life from which otherwise she was excluded. Then at age twenty-one Marguerite met a young teacher and spent a good deal of time with him. When he moved away from the city, he continued to visit her on various holidays. Her parents were vastly relieved, sup-

posing that marriage lay in her future. But after several years of
these sporadic visits, the teacher wrote to say that he had fallen in
love with another girl and that he planned to marry her.

Marguerite then became more recessive than before. Her mother
died, and she was left alone with her father. He, a staunch Catholic,
noted that her lassitude was beginning to affect her attention to
religious duties. He searched to find the cause of her lapse; but
not being well-equipped for understanding his daughter's problems, he blamed her withdrawal on the books in which she continually buried herself. He forbade her to continue with her
reading, and even burned some of the books he found in the house.

Soon after this happened, Marguerite began to take an inordinate
and uncharacteristic interest in her physical appearance. Hours
were spent in primping before her mirror. A never-ending shopping spree filled the house with new finery. Along with her mania
for clothes, Marguerite developed a delusion that she was pos-
sessed of an irresistible fascination for men. One glance at her and
a man was enslaved forever. Marguerite's father was shocked at
this frightening turn. He did what he could to control her, cancel-
ing her charge accounts and disposing of the more unsuitable
garments in her extensive new wardrobe. In turn, Marguerite
began to believe that she was pursued everywhere she went by
eager and potentially dangerous admirers. Even guests of the
family might be peremptorily accused of flirting with her.

The neurologist was asked to examine Marguerite. He noted
that her face invariably was held averted from him. Soon the
reason for this came out. She did not want the physician, as a
friend of the family, to be ensnared by her fatal beauty. The
physician could conclude from this only that Marguerite Ryan
was insane. And yet her insanity seemed to him to be truly a proof
of the balance struck by nature.

Deprived of physical beauty, the girl in her delusions had been
endowed generously with an imaginary charm. Thereby a state
which had been unbearable to live with had been remedied. Nature's purpose, believes the neurologist, is not so much to torture
the individual as to heal him. He offers the case of Marguerite
Ryan as evidence.

Ryan, Celeste Ryan, Marguerite Ryan.

"Nigger Jeff," 1901.

The City Editor of a large Midwestern newspaper assigns cub

reporter Elmer Davies to cover the purported rape of a nineteen-year-old girl, Ada Whitaker. The crime is reported from the small town of Pleasant Valley. The supposed rapist is Jeff Ingalls, a Negro. Because a posse led by Sheriff Mathews is hunting for Ingalls, and because the crime is one of a highly emotional nature, the City Editor suggests that a lynching—the first in the state—may be in the offing.

Davies travels to Pleasant Valley, which he finds seething with excitement. At the Whitaker farm, four miles from town, he interviews Mrs. Mathews, the Sheriff's wife. While at the farm he learns that Jeff Ingalls has been captured at his own home some distance along the main road. However, a gang of vigilantes intends to take him forcibly from the Sheriff's posse. With Davies as a spectator, the vigilantes confront the Sheriff and demand that the accused rapist be surrendered to them. Sheriff Mathews refuses.

When the Sheriff reaches the small village of Baldwin, his home, he takes Jeff Ingalls to his own cottage and places him under the guard of two deputies. The vigilantes approach again. This time Jake Whitaker, Ada's brother, is a member of the mob. Again the group is repulsed by the Sheriff. Davies is greatly encouraged by this action, enough so that he seeks out Seaver, the local telegraph operator, and files a lengthy story to his newspaper, headed "A Foiled Lynching."

But Davies' optimism proves to be premature. In the dark of night, near midnight, the vigilante band returns. This time Morgan Whitaker, Ada's father, has been recruited to lead the attack. Using Whitaker as a ruse to occupy the Sheriff, the mob rushes the cottage and manages to seize the prisoner. In a remote spot along the Pike River, Jeff is hanged.

On the following morning a puzzled and disturbed Elmer Davies makes his way to the Ingalls home. He interviews Jeff's young sister and learns from her that the boy's corpse has been returned to the family; a funeral is to be held on the following day. In a storage shed Davies comes upon the mother keening over her dead son's mutilated body. In this scene Davies feels the full extent of the tragedy.

Davies learns that it is the writer's job not to indict but to interpret. He determines to re-write his story of the lynching. He will incorporate everything he has learned and thereby do the tale full justice. So far as he is able, he must, in expressing his new aim, "get it all in!"

Elmer Davies, Jeff Ingalls, Sheriff Mathews, Mrs. Mathews, Seavey, Ada Whitaker, Jake Whitaker, Morgan Whitaker, Mrs. Morgan Whitaker.

"The Old Neighborhood," 1918.

The central figure of the story is an unnamed American industrialist engaged in revisiting the lower-income neighborhood in which he lived some twenty-four years previously with his wife Marie and their two young sons, Peter and Frank. He reflects on his past and his present.

Both he and Marie came from poor homes. In personality Marie was without force, a loving softness being her chief and most endearing trait. In contrast, her husband, a natural mechanic and incipient inventor, was driven by ambition. The couple were married when he was just twenty-four and beginning to realize that it was not entirely unrealistic for him to dream of huge projects and a prominent career in the burgeoning electrical industry. This ambition was threatened by his immediate responsibilities to his family.

First, Marie had fallen victim to a long and debilitating illness which drained the family's financial resources. Then, no sooner had she recovered than the couple's two young sons were taken ill. Both Peter and Frank died within three days of each other. At that time the boy's father was overwhelmed by a single ironical thought: was it to this sad end that he and Marie had been brought by their romantic dreams? If so, then he would have no more of them but henceforth would search for his happiness in material accomplishments. After the double tragedy he left Marie, abandoning her to whatever fate might have in store for her. Some years later, he was notified of her death.

Now, as this powerful business figure reminisces at age forty-eight, he cannot help comparing his present lot with his earlier status. He is an extremely rich man now, he commands hundreds of employees, he owns great shops and factories. With a new wife, a new family, he lives in an imposing mansion. Yet he cannot manage to drive the past from his mind. It is far too late, of course, for him to apologize for his neglect of Marie. The door to the past is tightly closed, and there is no chance to make amends.

He realizes now that ever since the day he left Marie he has been searching for a love as great and genuine and freely given as hers. He has not been successful in finding it. Now, when it is altogether

too late, he understands that his youth was crazed by the desire for
success, that for two decades and more he has been made the blind
victim of mad, illogical dreams and unworthy passions.   Life
assumes a dark aspect in his thinking.   People appear to fare no
better than the harried steers who are driven up a runway toward
their doom in a packing house.

In his old neighborhood the industrialist finds that, except for
an increased degree of dilapidation, most things remain quite
as he left them long ago.   Even the wallpaper in his former apartment appears to be the same.   But he realizes that his life can never
be what it once was.   He knows now that he will never fully overcome his deep sense of failure.   He will never be able to shrug off
the burden of guilt he carries for having abandoned Marie.   Life
has yielded him a truly great measure of material success, but in the
process it has rendered his existence meaningless.

Frank, Peter, Marie.

"Old Rogaum and His Theresa," 1901.

On New York's Bleeker Street, butcher Rogaum lives above his
shop with his wife and his daughter Theresa, just turned eighteen.
Her father keeps a watchful eye on Theresa, who recently has fallen
into the habit of walking out on the city streets of a summer night
with a group of girls from the surrounding neighborhood and not
returning until after the time established for her to be indoors.

Often the girls are joined by neighborhood boys such as "Connie"
Almerting and George Goujon.   At curfew time, Theresa is torn
between her acute infatuation for Connie and her deep sense of
obedience to her father.   He has threatened to lock the door of his
home against her if she persists in delaying her return past her ten
o'clock deadline.   One evening, lingering too long outside, Theresa
does find the door locked.   Rogaum is determined to teach her a
lesson.   He refuses to get up out of bed and unlock the door for her.

At Connie Almerting's suggestion that they take a stroll, Theresa
leaves the area, on the way encountering officers Maguire and
Delahanty, who recognize her.   As the night wears on, Rogaum, who
has not anticipated that his daughter might possibly leave the
relative security of their doorway, becomes concerned for her
safety, and dressing, he goes in search of her.   Near his butcher shop
he happens upon the body of a young woman, and for one shocking
moment he believes the corpse to be that of his Theresa.   When
Mrs. Rogaum arrives with a lamp, the two can see that the dead

girl's face is stained by an acid which she has drunk as a means of killing herself. They understand now the desperate end toward which they might be driving their Theresa, and they are overcome with remorse.

Officers Delahanty and Maguire investigate the suicide. They learn that Rogaum has locked Theresa out of his house. After chastising both Rogaums for their lack of wisdom, the policemen investigate the neighborhood brothel, where they discover that the dead girl is a prostitute named Annie. Originally she went on the streets after being locked out of her home by her parents. They determine to pass this news to Rogaum as an object lesson.

Descriptions of Theresa and Connie Almerting are placed on the police blotter. Officer Halsey, patrolling a neighborhood beat nearby, recalls having passed such a couple on the streets during his rounds. Before long the pair are located and taken to the precinct station. Rogaum is summoned and given a lecture on the hazards of setting his daughter on the city streets at such an hour. A wiser man now, yet no less determined to keep his daughter in check, Rogaum takes Theresa home, where she is welcomed by her relieved mother.

Adele, "Connie" Almerting, Officer Delahanty, Emily, George Goujon, Mrs. Kenrihan, Myrtle Kenrihan, Officer Maguire, Rogaum, Mrs. Rogaum, Theresa Rogaum.

"Phantom Gold," 1921.

The poverty-ridden farm country in which Bursay Queeder and his family exist is actually the nation's richest source of zinc. None of the area's inhabitants is aware of this. To them, the unsightly lumps of "slug" which litter their fields are worse than useless, for they must be hauled laboriously out of the way if the ground is to be cultivated.

These lumps, which the farmers use for fence building, actually are almost pure zinc, and soon after Judge Blow discovers that fact the region is deluged by prospectors who buy land and take options on farms. One day Cal Arnold, a neighbor of the Queeders, drops by with news that a nearby farm has been sold, by virtue of its "slug," for the seemingly exorbitant sum of $3,000. Bursay Queeder becomes interested in the possibility of selling his own place. His is a larger farm, and for that reason he speculates that $5,000 might perhaps be a fair price to ask for it. But he wants to keep all of the proceeds for himself, with nothing going to his wife or his son. To achieve this, he realizes that he will need to act in secret.

Before long a prospector, Crawford, arrives and strikes a bargain with Bursay Queeder. He will pay the farmer a down payment of $800 and the remainder, another $7,200, in sixty days. Queeder is ecstatic at the selling price: $8,000. His passion for cheating his wife of her due motivates Queeder to strike another bargain—a fictitious one—with Crawford. Mrs. Queeder is told that Crawford is to pay $100 down and the balance, $2,000, in sixty days. She believes the story and agrees to sell the farm on these terms. Crawford conspires with Bursay Queeder to pay him the larger sum surreptitiously, and in this manner it is anticipated that all parties concerned will be satisfied.

Queeder's son, Dode, hears a rumor that his father has sold the family farm for $5,000. He believes the tale, suspecting that his parents have connived to quote him the lower price as a means of deluding him. When he repeats the rumored price at home, Mrs. Queeder's suspicions are aroused also. As the days pass and the existence—and value—of the zinc deposits becomes better known, the prices of farms in the region rise sharply. The rumored prices of land soar even higher and faster, of course.

In such an atmosphere Bursay Queeder comes to believe that his farm should bring a good deal more than he has bargained for with Crawford. Yet he cannot admit this openly for fear of revealing the fraudulent nature of the $2,100 price he is supposed to have agreed to. Then a second zinc prospector arrives. He learns of the sale of the farm and advises Queeder to void his contract with Crawford on the basis that he did not understand the true significance of what he was selling. If Queeder is able to do this, the second prospector will pay him $25,000 for his land.

The temptation proves to be irresistible. When Crawford arrives in sixty days and asks to seal the bargain, Queeder refuses to go through with the sale. He accuses Crawford of attempting a swindle, and in an effort to win the family over to his side Crawford reveals that the true price he is paying is $8,000. This news arouses the fury of Dode, who threatens his father with physical violence if he fails to keep his end of the bargain. Mrs. Queeder and their daughter Jane back Dode. It is three against one. Bursay Queeder, although furious at the turnabout, signs the agreement of sale to Crawford.

The blow that life appears to have dealt him leaves Bursay

Queeder deranged. When he thinks of the second prospector's offer and what he has lost through his own greed, he goes out of his mind. Dode is full of plans for using the money from the sale. He ties his father up with a rope and assumes command.

> Cal Arnold, Judge Blow, Lester Botts, Crawford, Giles, Bursay Queeder, Mrs. Bursay (Emma) Queeder, Dode Queeder, Jane Queeder.

"The Prince Who Was a Thief," 1927.

In the Moslem city of Hodeidah the beggar storyteller Gazzar-al-Din hopes to earn a meal by telling the tale of a prince who was a thief. Finding a number of citizens willing to risk an anna on his talent, he proceeds with his story:

To Sultan Kar-Shem of the city of Yemen is born a son, Hussein. But the Sultan's rival, Bab-el-Bar, contrives to kidnap the child-prince and spirit him across the sands to Baghdad, where he is sold in bondage to Yussuf, a trainer of thieves. Hussein, now called Abou, being of a high native intelligence, proves a likely pupil. In time he becomes the favorite protégé of his master.

In Baghdad reigns the Caliph Yianko I, possessor of a great store of gold and the father of a beautiful daughter, Princess Yanee. One day the camel train bearing Yanee to her summer palace high in the mountains chances to pass the bazaar where Abou, in his master's absence, is in charge of Yussuf's carpet shop. As Abou gazes upon the beauty of Yanee, the princess reciprocates his interest fully. So handsome a sight is young Abou that the girl momentarily flings aside her veil in order that she might be better observed, and also in order that she might more readily observe Abou. Both young people fall in love. But neither at that moment knows the identity of the other.

When Yussuf returns, he brings explicit news of the Caliph Yianko's store of gold as well as an ingenious plan for robbing it. The two thieves, by artful cunning, manage to elude Yianko's guards. They come away from the treasury with considerable loot. For several nights thereafter they continue their depredations, but at last the Caliph's precautionary measures work and Yussuf is killed by falling into a bath of hot pitch. Abou, in order to prevent any identification of the corpse, severs Yussuf's head and takes it away with him.

Through a series of ruses, the Caliph attempts to outwit the thieves. But all of his tricks fail because of Abou-Hussein's superior mental capacities. In Yemen, meanwhile, the full truth concerning the abduction of Prince Hussein has at last been revealed. A search party comes to Baghdad and learns from Yussuf's widow that the child has been renamed Abou and is now a grown man. He is soon located. Once restored to his true position, Hussein contrives to win Yanee. The Caliph Yianko has made a public offer to grant his daughter's hand in marriage to the man who will deliver Abou the thief to him. In an ingenious charade, Hussein manages to reveal himself as being both prince and thief, and thereby he wins his beloved and achieves a happy ending for his story.

But Gazzar-al-Din, the beggar storyteller, is not able to achieve happiness for himself quite so easily. The scant handful of anna collected from his listeners does not add up to enough money to pay more than one-half of a day's support. Gazzar-al-Din is led to reflect upon the difficult path traveled by tellers of tales.

Abou (Hussein), Ajeeb, Gazzar-al-Din, Atrisha, Azad Bakht, Bhori, Chudi, Zad-el-Din, Feruz, Al Hadjaz, Haifa, Prince Hussein, Sultan Kar-Shem, Miriza, Waidi, Princess Yanee, Caliph Yianko I, Yussuf.

"The Shining Slave Makers," 1918. See "McEwen of the Shining Slave Makers."

"St. Columba and the River," 1925.

Dennis McGlathery is an immigrant Irish laborer. Despite a history of apparent bad luck in working near water, he signs up to join a crew which is cutting a traffic tunnel beneath the Hudson River. He will serve under a former boss, foreman Thomas Cavanaugh, and he will be paid a wage of five dollars a day, then an unheard-of sum for such work.

All goes well for seven months. Then a cave-in occurs which comes close to wiping out the entire crew of sand hogs. Once he reaches terra firma after this accident, McGlathery swears off this dangerous occupation forever. He has managed to save $600 in the bank and is planning to marry. He will not risk his life in this manner again, he decides.

Within a few years McGlathery has three children and is working for a daily wage of $1.50 rather than $5.00. He hears talk of a new and much safer method for tunneling which has made it feasible for contractors to think of resuming work on the Hudson tunnel. When the project does reopen, McGlathery, in spite of his former resolutions, joins the crew. First, however, he makes a visit to his parish church and petitions for the protection of St. Columba, patron saint of those working in connection with the earth's waters.

Again all goes well for several months. Then another accident occurs, this one killing foreman Cavanaugh. Again McGlathery has a miraculous escape; again he swears off this treacherous occupation forever. Five years after this, when McGlathery is the father of eight, work on the Hudson tunnel resumes once again. This time the crew is using a new safety device, called the "Great-head Shield." McGlathery, after considerable rumination, and after consulting seriously with St. Columba, rejoins the crew. This time he will be assistant to the foreman and earn $7.00 per day.

Again an accident occurs. In this one, McGlathery is blown out of the "Shield" and thrust upward to the river's surface, where an astounded tugboat captain pulls him from the water. In retrospect, McGlathery is convinced that St. Columba had placed the tugboat in this strategic position particularly in order to assure his timely rescue. He is carried back to the pressurized tunnel in order to cure the serious case of the bends that has resulted from his having popped to the surface so rapidly. Then he spends a number of weeks convalescing in the hospital.

McGlathery is left partially crippled from his accident. But the construction company offers him a substantial pension plus a generous cash bonus in return for his agreement not to sue for damages. Now McGlathery feels that St. Columba has truly done well in defending him against his archenemy, the river. Ever afterward, as he tells his story, he describes his escape as a genuine modern miracle.

> Thomas Cavanaugh, Henderson, Michael Laverty, Dennis
> McGlathery, Mrs. Dennis McGlathery, Patrick Murtha.

"Sanctuary," 1919.

The conditions under which Madeleine Kinsella has grown to age fifteen are dreadful. Her youth has been spent in dirty, crowded, smelly tenements set on stifling and dusty streets amid a human jungle of drunkenness, fighting, sickness, and death. But the miracle of miracle seems to have occurred; a flower apparently has managed to grow from a dung heap.

Madeleine's chronically unemployed father and her drunken mother have been no help at all to her. Like both her brother Frank and her sister Tina, Madeleine has had to go to work at an early age. Deflowered by a grocer's son and made pregnant by him, she becomes a prostitute in order to make her way in the world. She is duped by a plainclothes policeman who makes an assignation with her and then arrests her for soliciting.

Because she is a minor, Madeleine is sentenced to a year of confinement designed to correct her wayward behavior. Her caretakers, the Sisters of the Good Shepherd, put her to work at a machine in their sewing room. To Madeleine the nuns' convent represents a wholly new world, one of cleanliness and calm routine; it is an experience unlike any she has ever known. Gradually the convent becomes both her consolation and her security. The horror of her past life beyond these quiet walls gradually is forgotten.

Her year's sentence done, Madeleine is sent back into the world. She is somewhat better prepared, although not significantly so, to cope with life on the outside. For three years she finds it possible to work and support herself in some manner of decency. Then another handsome and careless youth is drawn to her by her beauty and her innocence, and he seduces her. After a travesty of a wedding she goes to live with him, confident that putting her trust in love has been the correct thing to do. But her euphoria is short lived. Madeleine's new lover, beset by gambling debts, persuades her to take up prostitution again; and a year later, when his debts are paid, he throws her out.

The beaten Madeleine can think of nowhere to turn except perhaps to the single spot on earth where she has ever known a small bit of peace. She finds her way to the Sisters of the Good Shepherd and begs the Mother Superior to take her into the convent, to allow her to work and to live there forever, and never to compel her to return to the outside world again. Mother St. Bertha, recognizing that Madeleine is unfit either by nature or by training to make her way alone and remain unscathed, agrees to her return.

Officer Amundsen, Nellie Fitzpatrick, Kinsella, Mrs. Kinsella, Frank Kinsella, Madeleine Kinsella, Viola Patters, Sister St. Agnes, Mother St. Bertha.

"The Second Choice," 1918.

In a dejected mood Shirley reviews her recent life and its import for her future. It makes a dark picture to contemplate. Until the handsome and glib Arthur Bristow came to town she had been not only content but also, she thought, happy as well. She lived with her parents in a very decent albeit very middle-class Midwestern neighborhood, and she was courted by the generous, hard-working Barton Williams, a man she seriously intended marrying.

But Arthur Bristow, with his good looks and fine ways, soon caused her to look upon her Bethune Street home as something decidedly second-rate, her neighborhood as mediocre or worse, and her fiancé as a country bumpkin lacking in any of the essential social graces. When Arthur asked Shirley to marry him, she thought that he meant it; she immediately gave up all thought of Barton. He no longer seemed in any fashion a suitable mate.

Instead, Shirley came to regard her romantic union with Arthur Bristow as an accomplished fact. She dreamed of someday moving with him to a far-off city, New York, perhaps, or San Francisco. After some months, during which she had refused Arthur nothing and had broken off entirely with Barton Williams, Shirley noticed that Arthur appeared to be losing interest in her. Before long he was called to a new job in Pittsburgh and was gone. Shirley has written him regularly there, but he has failed to respond. It seems obvious that he has no intention of encouraging their correspondence. Recently Shirley has written him one last, pathetic note. On its surface her letter asked that all of her messages to him be returned to her, but it was Shirley's hope that her request might cause Arthur to realize that he loved her.

Now her hopes seem to be dashed, for Arthur has written to say that he wishes to keep her letters as treasured mementos of their relationship. He promises to send her a postcard from Java, where a new assignment for his firm is taking him. All that the despondent Shirley can think of now is that her single chance to experience a great love has been ruined. She is driven to arranging a "chance" meeting with Barton Williams in the hope that he may become interested in her again. That she succeeds in this effort and that Barton takes immediate advantage of the opportunity, does little to cheer Shirley. Barton's obvious eagerness to pick up where they left off only serves to convince her more strongly of his commonness. Compared with the flashy Arthur, he seems more unworthy than ever.

For Shirley life has gone sour. Nothing will ever sweeten it again, she believes; and yet she cannot explain why it is that everything should have gone so terribly wrong. Life is a cruel mystery. A perversity seems to be at work: she loves Arthur, but he rejects her; she doesn't love Barton, and he crawls at her feet. To Shirley now, love seems no better than an impossible dream. She is certain that her loss of the fascinating Arthur will always color her life. She appears to be doomed by the uncaring forces of the universe never to achieve better than her second choice.

Arthur Bristow, Mabel Gove, Shirley, Barton Williams.

"The Shadow," 1924.

Beryl, against her better judgment, has married Gilbert, a clerk with lowly ambitions. After a year and a half of comparative happiness, the couple have a son, Gilbert, Jr., whom they nickname "Tickles." As the two lose their affection for each other, their love for Tickles grows ever stronger.

Gilbert is made jealous by a series of strange circumstances that arouse his suspicion of Beryl. He catches a glimpse of his wife riding in a strange automobile. Then he comes upon the ashes of a batch of mysterious letters unaccountably burned in his fireplace grate. Gradually he develops the belief that Beryl has fallen in love with a violinist, Raskoffsky. It dawns on him that she probably has been carrying on an affair with Raskoffsky for some time behind his back.

When at last Gilbert becomes sufficiently agitated to confront Beryl with his suspicions, she denies his interpretation vehemently. In her reaction, she implies that he must be losing his wits. Her convincing denial of the love affair with Raskoffsky stems from the fact that she has never had the slightest romantic interest in the violinist.

Beryl has, however, been involved in a love affair with a different man, a writer, Barclay. His novel *Heyday* centered on a girl whose story was strikingly similar to Beryl's own life. Feeling this rapport with the book, she wrote to Barclay; he replied, then paid her a visit, and for a few days Beryl had been in bliss. But the realities of life had intervened. Beryl has understood that in order to safeguard her marriage and thereby her relationship with her son, she must call a halt to the love affair. She has done so.

The end of her affair has been effected reluctantly, even bitterly, because she cannot help thinking it unfair that she must give up the novelist, whereas in Barclay's novel it had been the girl's husband who had gone away. The heroine of the novel had been left free to continue her romance. Life and fiction turn out to be two quite different things, and Beryl is helpless to change it.

Barclay, Alice Dana, Gilbert Stoddard, Mrs. Gilbert (Beryl Dana) Stoddard, Gilbert "Tickles" Stoddard, Jr.

Sister Carrie, 1900.

In 1889 Caroline Meeber, an inexperienced but alert and ambitious girl of eighteen, leaves her home in Columbia City, Wisconsin, and boards the train to seek her fortune in Chicago. A fellow passenger, Charles Drouet, a salesman, engages her in a lively conversation. Carrie is intrigued with Drouet. His apparent affluence impresses her most favorably. These two must part upon arriving in Chicago, but Drouet takes Carrie's address and promises to call on her.

Carrie goes to live with her sister Minnie and her husband, Sven Hanson, who rent a depressing apartment in a working-class neighborhood. Hanson cleans refrigerator cars at the stockyards for a living. He makes it clear that Carrie will be expected to find work and to contribute toward her board and room, but the girl is not successful in locating any job except in a sweatship making boys' caps at wages of $3.50 per week. She is so dejected at the sight of the place and the miserable wages that she continues searching; and when at last she locates a job in a small shoe factory at $4.50 per week, she feels that she has indeed made a grand start in Chicago after all. For the first time she is certain that she will find happiness in the city. But when her work proves to be extremely fatiguing and Drouet fails to call as he had promised to do, Carrie is once again dejected.

During an autumn rainy spell Carrie catches a bad cold and has to miss work, thereby losing her job. While in downtown Chicago searching for a new position, by chance she encounters Drouet. He escorts her to lunch at an expensive cafe and, hearing of her unemployed status, insists on helping to tide her over until she finds work. He gives her twenty dollars, which she does not refuse. It is enough to buy the warm clothes she needs for the coming winter. Overnight Carrie experiences second thoughts, but meeting Drouet again, she allows him to persuade her to accept a fine new coat and other attractive clothing.

Drouet wishes a more intimate relationship. On Wabash Avenue he rents a room for Carrie, presenting her to the landlady as his sister. Carrie understands that she is sliding rather dangerously far from the path her home training would indicate she follow, but she feels powerless to resist. She leaves a note on her pillow for Minnie and steals away quietly from the Hansons' to take up her new residence. She becomes Drouet's mistress and soon moves with him into a comfortable apartment at Ogden Place. She feels that she has risen a good distance in the world, a thought which pleases her.

Drouet's favorite place of recreation in Chicago is the popular saloon managed by George Hurstwood, a well-to-do friend. Encountering Hurstwood one evening in Fitzgerald and Moy's, Drouet invites the manager to visit in Ogden Place. Carrie is much impressed; in any comparison between the two men, Hurstwood in all respects outdistances Drouet. Hurstwood is a married man but feels a growing distance between himself and his wife. His children are relative strangers to him. He is attracted to Carrie, but at this time entertains little thought of initiating a romance. Carrie finds herself taking special pains with her appearance in order to achieve the approval of Hurstwood, and when the saloon manager discovers that she is not Drouet's wife he begins to consider the prospect of obtaining her for his own. He invites Drouet and Carrie to the theater, where he is noticed by a friend who unthinkingly mentions his presence there to Hurstwood's wife, a very suspicious woman.

Carrie, seeing more of Chicago, begins to think her place with Drouet not at all so grand as she once believed. The hope for something better takes possession of her mind. Before long Hurstwood declares his love openly; yet Carrie is not at all prepared to leave her secure position with Drouet for the uncertainty of an affair with him, however attractive he may be. Still, she does not rule Hurstwood out altogether; Drouet's failure to marry her suggests that their liaison may be only a temporary one. For a time, therefore, both men become important in Carrie's life.

While Drouet is away from the city on business trips, Carrie sees Hurstwood frequently. Drouet's branch of the Elks lodge sponsors an amateur theatrical production of "Under the Gaslight," and he persuades Carrie to try out for a role in it. She agrees and manages to win the part. In the process she reveals a natural but heretofore hidden talent for projecting her personality across the footlights. Hurstwood, attending the play, falls more in love with Carrie than ever, and he continues to make advances which she feels she must resist.

In the meanwhile Hurstwood's home life is deteriorating rapidly. Mrs. Hurstwood hears reports of his being seen at various spots in Chicago with a younger woman, and she learns that in attending the Elks play he lied about her absence, pleading that she had remained home because of an illness. Without actually intending to do it, Hurstwood breaks with his wife during the course of a particularly vigorous family quarrel, and as their estrangement deepens, Mrs. Hurstwood threatens to create a damaging scandal by suing him for divorce. Her condition for exercising restraint calls for him to deliver the bulk of his property into her hands.

Upon being handed an ultimatum by his wife's attorneys, Hurstwood becomes desperate. That night as he is closing up at Fitzgerald and Moy's he discovers that the safe has been left unlocked and a delivery of some ten thousand dollars from the bank not put away. The temptation to steal the money is great. Hurstwood vacillates. Eventually he chances to jar the safe door closed while the money is in his hands; he feels now that he must take it, for to explain his possession of it in the morning would be too painful an embarrassment. He calls on Carrie, convinces her that Drouet has been hospitalized on the South Side and that he is to take her to him, and within the hour the two are on a train, bound for Detroit and then for Montreal.

Carrie allows herself to be swept into Hurstwood's plans. His promise of eventual marriage soothes any qualms she might otherwise feel. When detectives follow Hurstwood to Montreal, he returns the bulk of his embezzled money, retains $1,300 for a new start for himself, and takes Carrie to New York, where they live under the pseudonym of Wheeler. Hurstwood uses his money to purchase a one-third interest in a saloon. For two years all goes well. The couple live in a fine apartment on Seventh-eighth Street, and Carrie becomes fast friends with her prosperous neighbor, Mrs. Vance.

Together with Mrs. Vance, and sometimes with both Vances and their friend Robert Ames as well, Carrie sees a good deal of New York. The perennial display of affluence informs her that her situation with Hurstwood is in no way so advantageous as she originally believed it to be. She begins to yearn for finer things and the money that would make them hers. But instead of moving upward, Carrie retrogresses, for Hurstwood's saloon does not prove to pay so well as he anticipated, and he moves Carrie to an apartment farther downtown at Thirteenth Street. It is so much less desirable an address that she feels ashamed even to let the Vances know where she lives.

Then the owner of the building housing Hurstwood's saloon is sold and he finds himself out of business entirely. A financial panic is underway in the nation, and when his capital vanishes overnight, Hurstwood becomes one of thousands of unemployed men. A middle-aged person such as himself is hard put to find any kind of decent work. He begins a process of many months of slow deterioration. His remaining funds, although guarded carefully, dribble away dollar by dollar. He is reduced to spending his days loitering in public lobbies of hotels.

Carrie is alarmed for her security. Hurstwood's idleness motivates her to seek work for herself. She recalls her minor success in the Elks lodge play and tries the Broadway theaters, eventually locating work as a chorus girl. As Carrie Madenda she begins a minor theatrical career. A more experienced friend, Lola Osborne, befriends her and serves as her mentor in locating better roles. After appearing in a show or two, Carrie is able to command a somewhat better salary, and so she rises, slowly but surely.

Hurstwood, in contrast, continues to decline. Even his personal appearance, once impeccable, deteriorates sadly. Before long his meager savings have been exhausted, and Carrie must contribute more and more to the running of their house. Hurstwood takes a job running a streetcar during a strike in Brooklyn; the strike takes an ugly tone, he is abused as a scab and shot at. While the bullet does no more than graze his flesh, the experience is shattering enough to send him back to Manhattan even more frightened than before. His survival is clearly in jeopardy.

Carrie meanwhile has achieved a small speaking part on the stage, a distinct advance. She can sense the possibility of an interesting career ahead. While driving to secure it she is unwilling to burden herself with the support of Hurstwood, for whom she no longer has any genuine affection. Leaving him twenty dollars and a farewell note, she moves out and takes an apartment with her actress friend Lola Osborne. In time Carrie becomes a celebrity of the American stage. Her theatrical roles improve vastly, her salary rises rapidly, hotels are eager to provide her with special rates purely because of the publicity—and thus the patronage—which her presence attracts. She is sought after by wealthy men, and she re-establishes her friendship with the Vances.

But Hurstwood goes from bad to worse. Only a few dollars separate him from starvation. He sleeps in a Bowery flophouse and eventually is reduced to panhandling in the city streets. Noticing a newspaper report of Carrie's show returning to New York, he goes to her theater and begs directly from her. His appearance and demeanor are an embarrassment to her now, and she gives him money in order to be rid of him. Drouet returns also, drawn by the widespread publicity concerning Carrie's success on the stage. But Carrie by now has far outdistanced the salesman and feels that she has nothing in common with him any more.

Once again Carrie meets the Vances' friend Robert Ames. His intellectual qualities appeal to her; he is something different from anything she has known heretofore. He appears to be pointing something out to her, something beyond and above the station she has now attained. Ames is clearly disappointed that Carrie has never pushed her limits sufficiently to attempt more serious stage roles than those in musical comedy. He advises that she try a comedy drama, then perhaps a straight dramatic play. She wonders whether he might not be correct. Perhaps true greatness lies just ahead, beyond the immediate horizon, waiting for her.

Hurstwood inevitably is driven to the wall. In despair he commits suicide by turning on the gas jets in a flophouse cubicle. His body is born anonymously to Potter's Field for burial with other paupers. By contrast, Carrie, for one glorious moment supremely happy in her musical-comedy success, is now restless again. True happiness has eluded her. Wealthy, pampered, sought after, yet she is unsatisfied. She cannot forget what Ames has told her, cannot avoid pondering over his words. Perhaps up ahead somewhere, if she can earn enough money to underwrite the effort, there lies a career that will end in genuine and lasting fulfillment, something to provide her life with import. But is Robert Ames correct? She wonders. Life is a puzzle.

Robert Ames, Bamberger, Dr. Beale, Mrs. Bermudez, Cargill, Charles H. Drouet, Frank A. Hale, Mrs. Frank A. Hale, Sven C. Hanson, Mrs. Sven C. (Minnie) Hanson, Mrs. Hoaglund, George W. Hurstwood, Mrs. George W. (Julia) Hurstwood, George W. Hurstwood, Jr., Jessica Hurstwood, Kenny, Carrie Madenda (Caroline Meeber), Harry McGarren, Caroline "Carrie" Meeber, Millice, Mrs. Morgan, Sagar Morison, G.W. Murdock (George W. Hurstwood), Mrs. G. W. Murdock (Caroline Meeber), Oeslogge, Lola Osborne, Harry Quincel, Shaughnessy, Frank L. Taintor, Bart Taylor, Vance, Mrs. Vance, G. W. Wheeler (George W. Hurstwood), Mrs. G. W. Wheeler (Caroline Meeber), Withers.

The Stoic, 1947.
Frank Algernon Cowperwood, having been defeated in his bid to

obtain long-term franchises for his Chicago streetcar lines in 1898, determines to sell his Midwestern properties and move on to a more receptive location. He has in mind London, where a rare opportunity exists in the transit field. The Traffic Electrical Company, having obtained a franchise to extend a subway from Charing Cross to Hampstead, has run out of money and needs a large investor. Cowperwood sends his deputy Henry de Sota Sippens to London to scout out this property and determine whether it might be an appropriate first step for his employer.

Unable to divest himself of his second wife, Aileen, Cowperwood has taken the beautiful and youthful Berenice Fleming as his mistress. She exacts a promise that he will curb his habitual and flagrant promiscuity and devote himself wholly to her. Cowperwood, although for many years he has not been without lovers, agrees to this condition. At Berenice's instigation Cowperwood attempts to solve the problem of Aileen by employing a handsome ne'er-do-well, Bruce Tollifer, to divert his wife's attention.

Sippens in London quickly determines that the existing subways, the Metropolitan and District lines, comprise a loop similar to that which gave Cowperwood an advantage over his rivals in Chicago. If somehow he can gain control of these two lines and add to them the projected Charing Cross-Hampstead line, Cowperwood will be in a commanding position. When he learns from Greaves and Henshaw, representatives of Traffic Electrical, that the firm is in trouble financially, Cowperwood plans to go to London to survey the situation for himself.

It is arranged for Frank and Aileen Cowperwood to sail on the *Kaiser Wilhelm der Grosse*; Bruce Tollifer is to be aboard, assigned responsibility for winning Aileen's attention. Sailing ahead of the *Kaiser Wilhelm*, on the *Saxonia*, is Berenice Fleming, in the company of her mother. At Pryor's Cove along the Thames River not far from Windsor, Cowperwood leases an estate for Berenice, a retreat to which he may legitimately come under the guise of visitor. The estate is the property of Lord Stane, one of the largest shareholders in London transit companies, a man whom Cowperwood must bring into his fold if he hopes to gain control of the underground system.

In order to allay any suspicions Aileen might have, Cowperwood makes a pretense of great affection for her, simultaneously encouraging Tollifer, now in Paris at Cowperwood's instructions, to ask Aileen to meet him there. With his wife safely on the Continent, Cowperwood takes Berenice on a tour of the English cathe-

dral towns. In Paris, Tollifer arranges for Aileen to be continually
entertained. Under his tutelage she happily agrees to drink less,
reduce her weight, and patronize the greatest of Parisian couturi-
ères. In London, Cowperwood makes Lord Stane's acquaintance
and professes an interest in obtaining a directorial rather than a
personal control of the underground system in which Stane has
large interests. Actually, Cowperwood intends the opposite; he
fully expects to maintain and personally command the transit
system, including a metropolitan loop, and to use it against rival
underground lines as a means of bringing them to their knees
so that he might eventually absorb them as well and become sole
dictator of London subways.

In order to finance his huge plan, Cowperwood needs more
money than he can raise by himself. He returns to New York in
order to promote funds. On his way he stops in Paris and asks
Aileen to accompany him, this in order to prevent her from suspecting any deception on his part. Berenice during this time is to
remain in England. Cowperwood and Aileen return to America,
Bruce Tollifer following on another boat. Cowperwood pays flying
visits to financial centers such as Chicago, Boston, and Philadelphia
in search of investors, with good success.

While Cowperwood is in Baltimore a young dancer, Lorna Maris,
visits his hotel and introduces herself as being, in actuality, a Cowperwood, albeit a rather distant relative, Frank's father and her
grandfather having been brothers. The two are mutually attracted
and become lovers. When the scandal sheet *Town Topics* prints
an account of Cowperwood's dalliance, Aileen sees it and sends a
copy anonymously to Berenice Fleming. Eventually this copy is
forwarded to her at Pryor's Cove. The news is doubly disturbing,
since Berenice already is contemplating the obvious fact that Lord
Stane is attracted to her and that she is attracted both to him and
to his social station in England.

Berenice begins to question whether her loyalty to Cowperwood,
now sixty years old, is well placed. Stane has invited her to his
estate, Tregesal, and she has protested that it is necessary for her
to obtain Cowperwood's assent before going. But now, angry at
Frank's deception, she plans to visit Tregesal without waiting for
word from him. Cowperwood senses that Berenice's silence reflects
her probable awareness of the *Town Topics* gossip; he determines
to end his affair with Lorna Maris. With Aileen he returns to
England. He confesses openly to Berenice and promises that in the

future he will attempt to be faithful to her; she admits that between him and Lord Stane, Frank is the more attractive man. They
are reconciled.

Quietly Cowperwood proceeds with his plan to buy up London
subways. Once he has put together his grand monopoly, he proposes
to sell out at an immense profit and retire while his reputation and
achievement stand at their peak. But his entry into London transportation has made others aware of potential profits to be made
there. In particular, Stanford Drake, a great American financier,
enters the field as Cowperwood's rival, with a plan to construct
lines paralleling the Cowperwood system. Each organization
petitions Parliament for a franchise; but the question is decided in
favor of Cowperwood, and Stanford Drake withdraws, beaten.

Aileen visits Paris and Bruce Tollifer again. At a party, Tollifer's
girl friend, Marigold Brainerd, who is jealous and has had too much
to drink, inadvertently reveals to Aileen enough of the truth of
Tollifer's position for her to guess that he is in essence a hired
gigolo. She is infuriated both at Tollifer and at her husband, and
she dismisses the paid escort. Meanwhile, with Aileen away, Cowperwood has accepted an invitation to cruise with Stane on his
yacht with a number of other guests, including, by design, Berenice
Fleming. Aileen returns to New York, leaving a letter for her
husband in which she threatens to expose him in the public press.
Since a scandal would prove to be most awkward for his intricate
business dealings just now, Frank follows her to America in the
guise of repentance and manages to make a temporary peace with
her.

Frank Cowperwood's collection of art by now has become recognized as being one of the foremost in the world. Because his mansion on Fifth Avenue in New York has been designed for eventual
use as a gallery but cannot conveniently contain his hoard of paintings, statuary, and rare tapestries, Cowperwood purchases the
adjoining home and puts Aileen in charge of remodeling it into a
second gallery. Thus flattered, Aileen becomes acquiescent once
more. It is essential that Frank return to his negotiations in England, and Aileen approves his sailing.

Once reaching London, Cowperwood leaves with Berenice on
a rented yacht for a tour of the Norwegian fjords. His health has
begun to decline, but during the vacation he regains his old vigor
sufficiently to carry on the strenuous schedule required to put his
monopoly together. He looks forward to the inevitable, however,

and determines to commission a magnificent tomb which will be ready when the time comes to receive his body and also Aileen's. A London specialist, Dr. Wayne, examining Cowperwood, informs him that he has Bright's disease and that in all probability he has no more than a year to live.

Secretly, Cowperwood begins making plans for his business and personal affairs to be taken care of. He does not inform Berenice of the seriousness of his illness; but when the two of them attend a social affair in his honor at Tregesal, he is stricken. During his recovery he sends for his American physician, Dr. James, who, arriving in England, confirms the diagnosis of Bright's disease. Dr. James nurses his patient back to temporary health. Cowperwood is able to vacation on the Continent, an act which helps him to confound the rumors of his ill health and imminent demise which have circulated in London and even appeared in the press.

He proceeds with his underground project and hurries the building of his marble tomb in Brooklyn. Five months after recovering from his first serious attack, he is stricken once again. This time he realizes that the end is near. He sails for New York, bidding Berenice Fleming to follow on the next boat. During the ocean voyage Cowperwood suffers another bad attack, and in New York he must be carried from the boat by stretcher.

An ambulance takes Cowperwood, not to his mansion, now being remodeled to receive its new gallery, but to the Waldorf Astoria. Berenice receives news of his illness while still at sea. She rushes to the hotel upon her disembarkation and vows to remain close to her lover throughout his illness. Aileen has hardened herself against her unfaithful husband, but when she learns that his illness is terminal she relents. Their reconciliation is spoiled when Aileen learns that Berenice Fleming is in residence at the Waldorf also. Frank has duped her once again.

Cowperwood dies, and the bitter Aileen refuses to allow his coffin into the mansion for its lying in state. The financier's underlings, intent even now on preserving a facade of respectability, bribe his servants to open the Fifth Avenue doors, and Cowperwood is borne home in the dark of night. The imposing tomb in Greenwood Cemetery has been completed in time, and the financier is interred there.

Berenice Fleming returns to the grand home on Park Avenue which Frank Cowperwood gave her. She is shocked to see her relations with the financier exposed by every newspaper in the city. Cowperwood's demise has shaken her badly; it brings her face to face with the mystery of existence. Frank's earthly grandeur seems to have perished utterly. What has it all meant, her life and his? Berenice determines to visit India and investigate the philosophy of the Yogis, believing thereby to achieve the answers she seeks and does not find elsewhere.

Frank Cowperwood's will provides for generous bequests to the financier's family. His art collection will be given to the City of New York, and another generous sum is to be spent in building a Cowperwood Hospital for the needy. Thus does the financier hope to achieve his immortality. But these plans are stalled when one creditor after another goes to court in order to press suits against the estate. For five years Aileen is led through a maze of litigation whose upshot is to drain the estate of its assets. Eventually, in order to obtain her widow's share, Aileen is compelled to leave the mansion. It and the art collection are put on the auction block and sold.

Not long afterward Aileen herself dies, officially of pneumonia, but actually, says her physician, of grief caused by her many troubles. In India, Berenice Fleming is so affected by her study of Indian philosophy as to be converted wholly from her former narcissism. She rejects the materialistic way of life she has followed and determines instead to sell the mansion, the jewels, and the other treasures which Cowperwood showered upon her. With the proceeds she will erect the great hospital he planned to build.

[At this point *The Stoic*, as Dreiser wrote it, comes to an end. In an appendix constructed by Helen Richardson Dreiser, Berenice makes the Cowperwood Hospital a reality and devotes herself to a life of labor with the neglected children of the poor who are brought there for treatment. In this manner she aspires to amend her life and to achieve a redeeming spirituality.]

Horace Albertson, Sir Humphrey Babbs, Ibrihim Abbas Bey, Edward Bingham, Blandish, Guru Borodandaj, Lady Bosvike, Lord Bosvike, Mrs. Sidney (Marigold Shoemaker) Brainerd, Oliver Bristol, Bullock, Calthorpe, Dr. Camden, Buckner Carr, Mrs. Ira George Carter, Rolfe Carter, Byron Chance, Lady Clifford, Raphael Cole, Lord Colvay, C. B. Courtright, Frank Algernon Cowperwood, Mrs. Frank Algernon (Aileen Butler) Cowperwood, Frank Algernon Cowperwood, Jr., William H. Cunningham, Cuthbert, Charles Day, Delafield, Denton, Dickson (Frank Algernon Cowperwood), Sir Hudspeth Dighton, Dolan, J. L. Donahue, Stanford Drake, William Edmunds, Lady Ettinge, Lord Ettinge, Mrs. Evans, Berenice Fleming, Frederickson,

Alassandra Givens, Montague Greaves, Grelizan, Lord
Haddonfield, Caroline Hand, Eric Hansen, Rosalie Har-
rigan, Hartley, Constance Hathaway, Colonel Hawkesberry,
Philip Henshaw, Dr. Jefferson James, Albert Jamieson,
William Jarkins, Sir Wilmington Jeems, Elverson Johnson,
Kitteredge, Willem Kloorfain, Leeks, Rexford Lynnwood,
Duchess of Marlborough, Lorna Maris, Dr. Middleton,
Ostade, Raymond Pyne, Randolph, Maria Reystadt, Wel-
lington Rider, Judge Roberts, Robertson, Rose, Victor
Leon Sabinal, Abbington Scarr, Heinrich Schreiber, Lord
Severence, Judge Severing, Michael Shanley, Marigold
Shoemaker (Mrs. Sidney Brainerd), Henry de Sota Sippens,
Speyer, Gordon Roderick Lord Stane, Reverend Willis
Steele, Sir Charles Stoneledge, Wilson Styles, Arthur Tavi-
stock, Mrs. Anna Templeton (Lillian Cowperwood), Mrs.
Judith Thorne, Lord Tilton, Bruce Tollifer, Colonel Wex-
ford Tollifer, Kathryn Trent (Berenice Fleming), Warburton, Arlette Wayne, Dr. Wayne, Mrs. Anna (Lillian Semple Cowperwood) Wheeler, Sir Wyndham Whitley, Wyndham Willets, Williams.

"A Story of Stories," 1918.

In a Western city of the United States live two rival newspapermen.
One is David Kolinsky of *The News*, a Jew who so strongly resembles a red-headed Irishman in appearance that he adopts the pen
name of "Red" Collins. Collins is a showy dresser who possesses a
brash, self-confident manner. On the city's other paper, *The Star*,
works Augustus Binns, considerably more sedate in demeanor,
rather collegiate and literary in manner. He considers himself a
cut above Collins in most respects.

Since *The News* is the more prestigious of the city's papers,
one might wonder how it should happen that the brash Collins
would be its leading reporter, while the more decorous Binns
works for the second-best sheet. The answer is this: the city editor
of *The News*, Batsford, a Westerner, was resentful of the sophistication of Binns, an Easterner. He had required him to serve as
rewrite man for stories originally filed by the knowledgeable but
semi-literate Collins. At last, in order to preserve his self-respect
against this and other indignities, Binns had angrily resigned and
gone over to *The Star*.

From their respective positions on the two papers, the reporters
continue to compete. Binns, who is the more able and inquisitive

writer, usually has the advantage in this contest. One day news arrives of the arrest of Lem Rollins, who has been sought as one of seven bandits who some months past purportedly held up the train carrying the Governor and his staff. But Rollins, in his confession to lawmen, is said to have made a claim that he worked alone. If this be true, it makes liars of the Governor and members of his military staff who swore that it had taken seven heavily armed men to carry out the $30,000 robbery of the train.

To get the facts, Binns travels to Pacific, a junction point at which he can join the train which is carrying Rollins back to justice. He recognizes the story as being potentially a very big one; he is determined to get the jump on his rival, Collins, and on all other reporters as well. But when he arrives in Pacific, he finds that Collins is there already. Collins searches for Rollins on one arriving express, mistakenly. Binns meanwhile runs to the second railroad station in the town and bribes the station master to stop the train which actually is carrying the bandit.

His ploy fails, however, when Collins reaches the second train in time to climb aboard and become the first to locate the prisoner. As they all ride home together, Rollins' true story emerges. He is a freight handler by profession, but for many months he was laid off by the railroad and unable to find other employment. In his work he became privy to the methods used by the railroad in shipping money across country. Newspaper stories had informed him in some detail of methods employed by bandits. On these two type of information he was able to plan his coup all by himself, without needing other help.

The holdup occurred in the dark of night. Rollins' occasional pistol shots and the shouts he aimed at imaginary cohorts created the impression among the passengers that a band of several robbers was at work. His success was spoiled only by his carelessness in leaving at the scene of the crime a bag containing a handkerchief whose intitials could be traced to his girl friend. Binns and Collins, hearing this recital, recognize that they have a sensational piece of news here, truly a story of stories.

Binns is resigned to sharing the story with his rival, Collins, albeit reluctantly. But he balks when Collins suggests that they take the bandit to the offices of his *News* for photographs. He relents only when it is pointed out to him that *The News* building is closer and better equipped for flash pictures. Collins' suggestion is adopted.

Binns is beaten finally when he realizes too late that Collins plans

a photograph all too clearly situated in the editorial offices of
The News and that the bandit will be surrounded by *News* reporters and editors.   Such a photograph will clearly be unusable
by the rival *Star*.   Once again craftiness has triumphed over quality.
Binns berates himself for his own failure to anticipate the ploy and
to take whatever measures, ethical or otherwise, might have
prevented Collins from scoring such a coup.

   Batsford, Augustus Binns, David "Red" Collins (David Kol-
   linsky), Lem Rollins, Waxby.

The Titan, 1914.
   Frank Algernon Cowperwood, having regained his freedom and
his fortune in Philadelphia after his 1871 conviction for embezzlement, sets out for Chicago in search of a new field in which to pursue his business interests.   As soon as he sees the raw city on the
shore of Lake Michigan, its suburbs growing at an unprecedented
rate, he knows that he has a rare opportunity.   He dreams of con-
trolling a vast network of streetcar lines that will monopolize urban
transportation in Chicago.
   Cowperwood is armed with a letter of introduction to Judah
Addison, a Chicago bank president and civic leader who brings him
together with Timothy Arneel, the meat packer, and Anson Merrill, the city's leading dry-goods merchant.   In order to establish
a solid friendship, Cowperwood confides in Addison the facts of
his embezzlement conviction and his plans for divorce.   Then,
convinced that Chicago is the place he wishes to locate in, he
returns to Philadelphia for Aileen Butler.   She is captivated by
Chicago and dreams of the grand life which will be hers when
she is married to her lover and securely established in society.
His divorce granted, Cowperwood marries Aileen and they settle
in Chicago.
   Cowperwood establishes a business in partnership with Peter
Laughlin, a member of the Chicago Board of Trade; and with
Laughlin's help he enters the public utilities field more or less
unnoticed and purchases a group of small suburban gas companies.
Each of these firms owns a service franchise, unimportant sep-
arately, but in conjunction forming a small monopoly, a very effective tool with which to harass the larger and more complacent
public-utility firms.   He begins to employ men who can be helpful
to him and will be his faithful minions in future enterprises:
Henry De Soto Sippens, General Judson P. Van Sickle, and Kent

Barrows McKibben. With these men to supply the intimate knowledge of Chicago which he does not possess, Cowperwood sets out to effect his first financial coup.

The aid of Chicago's most powerful political boss, John J. McKenty, is enlisted in support of Cowperwood. With McKenty's support and advice Frank feels adequate to rebuffing the representative of the major gas companies, financier Norman Schryhart, who proposes to buy out the Cowperwood combine for a paltry sum. In the end, the gas companies have no choice but to settle at Cowperwood's price. Even after making generous payments to his henchmen and his partner, Cowperwood is left with a princely sum of money with which to advance upon his true target, the city's street railways.

Frank Cowperwood's success is not accomplished without a price. The civic leaders who cannot best him in finance find him vulnerable socially. He builds a grand home on Michigan Avenue, only to discover that none of the important Chicagoans whose approbation he covets are willing to attend his entertainments. The wives of the great merchants and meatpackers find Aileen overly colorful, vulgar, and too dangerously beautiful to be acceptable within their ranks. The truth of her past relationship with Cowperwood spreads rapidly, and before long she and Frank are social outcasts in the city whose domination they anticipated. Frank blames Aileen for their predicament, and even though he at first determines to remain faithful to her the foundations of their marriage weaken. For diversion the Cowperwoods travel abroad. Frank works at assembling a noteworthy collection of paintings and sculpture.

Other women catch Frank Cowperwood's eye. Notable among the group is Rita Sohlberg, beautiful young wife of a Danish violinist. The Cowperwoods and the Sohlbergs are friends, and for more than a year neither Aileen nor Harold Sohlberg suspects that their spouses are lovers. Once his fidelity to Aileen is broken, Cowperwood's sexual varietism is unbridled; even while involved with Rita, he initiates an affair with a stenographer, Antoinette Nowak. By happenstance Aileen discovers the existence of Antoinette and hires detectives to pursue the case. To Aileen's infinite distress they uncover the fact that Rita Sohlberg is Frank's mistress. When Rita next calls at the Cowperwood mansion Aileen attacks her physically, inflicting serious damage, and only Frank's timely intervention saves Rita from mutilation. Although her husband's affair with Rita is ended, Aileen knows that her marriage is in serious difficulty.

The Cowperwood business affairs, on the other hand, could scarcely go better. Frank initiates his move to control street railways when he notes that the North Chicago City Railway is ripe for a purchase. It has stagnated because its access to the downtown areas is hampered by the Chicago River. A long-unused tunnel beneath the river exists, one built by the city at great cost in former years but used only briefly because of engineering difficulties. Cowperwood observes that the tunnel might easily be revamped to accommodate streetcars. He first moves to procure the North Chicago Company. He then secures, at an extremely favorable rate, rights to the tunnel and a franchise extending his new line directly into the central shopping district of the city.

In all of this Cowperwood has been aided by his political henchmen, who show him the fastest route through the Chicago City Council: bribery. But he is opposed by the majority of metropolitan newspapers, who call his tunnel deal an example of open theft and berate not only him but the cooperating aldermen as well. Only one paper, the *Press*, edited by Augustus Haguenin, is friendly to the Cowperwood interests. Before long Cowperwood adds the Chicago West Division Company to his possessions, procures rights to another disused tunnel, that under Washington Street, brings the new line in to join his downtown loop, and is well on his way to control of Chicago transit.

On a trip abroad the Cowperwoods meet the beautiful Stephanie Platow, nineteen-year-old daughter of a Chicago furrier, and after their return Aileen continues the acquaintance. Stephanie becomes a prominent member of the local Little Theatre group, the "Garrick Players," and has love affairs with two members of this group, first with Gardner Knowles, dramatic critic of the *Press*, and then with Lane Cross, the artist who serves the group as stage director. The Cowperwoods attend the performance of "Elektra" in which Stephanie appears.

Frank Cowperwood's attention is caught by Stephanie Platow. Soon they become lovers. But while Frank routinely accepts his own sexual varietism, he is appalled at promiscuity in his mistresses and, suspecting Stephanie, puts an employee on her trail. One night, cued for the occasion, Cowperwood comes upon her making love with a new member of the Garrick Players, Forbes Gurney, in the studio of Lane Cross. Their association ends with this exposure. Cowperwood continues to have his affairs; a variety of women attract him, but one of his choices proves unfortunate: Cecily Haguenin, daughter of his supporter on the *Press*. When Cecily's father discovers his daughter's seduction, he breaks with Cowperwood.

Aileen Cowperwood, as a release for her own frustration and also in order to spite her husband, casts her lot socially with a group of hangers-on in the art world, notably Polk Lynde, who is intent upon initiating an affair with her. Another dangerous enemy for Cowperwood is created when Frank seduces Caroline Hand, young wife of a Chicago financier, Hosmer Hand. Along with Timothy Arneel and Norman Schryhart, Hand operates the Chicago City Railway, rival of the Cowperwood lines, and now he is doubly motivated to injure Cowperwood whenever and wherever possible.

As aids to his monopolistic ambitions, Cowperwood purchases the services of two powerful aldermen, Michael Tiernan and Patrick Kerrigan, political lords of the first and second wards in Chicago and men in a good position to deliver the Chicago City Council to the Cowperwood interests. Receiving a temporary set-back in city-wide elections, Cowperwood attempts to suborn the newly elected Mayor, Chaffee Thayer Sluss, and not succeeding at first, contrives the Mayor's seduction by a hired agent, Claudia Carlstadt, who secures letters with which to blackmail him. By this means Cowperwood is able to silence the Mayor's intended opposition to his drive for long-term streetcar franchises.

On a trip to Louisville, Kentucky, Cowperwood is taken to a society brothel operated by one Hattie Starr, a widow once socially prominent but now fallen upon hard times. He sees a photograph of Hattie Starr's beautiful young daughter, Berenice Fleming, and falls half in love. The process is completed when he meets Berenice in person and rapidly comes to believe that with this beauty at his side he might achieve the conquest of society which until now has been withheld from him. Since Berenice is still in her teens, Cowperwood arranges for her education, planning ahead for the time when he might make her his own.

When public opposition in Chicago rises against him, Frank Cowperwood begins a series of civic benefactions. The most prominent of these is the gift of a costly telescope, the largest in the world, to the University of Chicago. But the positive effect of this is mitigated soon afterward when he begins to erect a new mansion for himself on Millionaires Row along Fifth Avenue, New York, and it becomes evident that sooner or later he will leave the Midwest.

Aileen's affair with Polk Lynde fails, her heart never really being in it. She takes to heavy drinking and initiates another sordid affair, this time with a sculptor, Watson Skeet. Cowperwood is appalled at the manner in which Aileen has degraded herself; yet he takes no blame for her plight and does not discourage her affairs, since having Aileen so occupied leaves him relatively free to live his own private life as he sees fit.

By 1896 Cowperwood's financial power has grown so large that his rivals are eager to bring him down by whatever means possible. A monopoly of the match industry is attempted by Hosmer Hand, Norman Schryhart, Timothy Arneel, and Anson Merrill when they back the "American Match" stock promoted by Phineas Hull and Benoni Stackpole. When the stock is involved in a selling panic, Cowperwood's rivals purchase as much as they are able in order to protect their investment. But a time comes when they cannot buy further. Hull and Stackpole then approach Cowperwood with fifteen thousand shares which they offer as collateral for a loan to tide them over their crisis.

Cowperwood makes the loan, not directly, but through friends who owe him favors. His plan is to feed the Match stock out in small lots, to force his rivals to pick it up, and then as the price sinks to buy it back himself. Thus he will profit twice over. His plan succeeds, and his rivals are pushed to extreme measures to purchase the stock when it floods the market. Learning that Stackpole and Hull have approached Cowperwood, Arneel and the others suspect the truth. They plot to ruin Cowperwood by pressuring local banks to call at once his considerable loans. But their plot backfires when Cowperwood, rather than capitulate to their demands, threatens instead to call the loans his friends have made to Stackpole and Hull. He will dump his Match stock on an already glutted market and thereby create a financial panic that will ruin his rivals. They choose the less expensive route of allowing American Match to fail.

This coup marks the peak of Cowperwood's success in Chicago. He has defeated his rivals, and his wish to possess Berenice Fleming becomes a realistic possibility when her mother's past is revealed and her chances for a society marriage vanish. All that Frank needs now is a set of long-term franchises which will assure the prosperity of his streetcar lines in years to come and thereby make of them a marketable commodity which can be sold at an immense profit. He looks forward to moving to New York, a millionaire many times over. He succeeds in having the Illinois state legislature approve his franchises, but when he attempts to bribe Governor Swanson and prevent a veto, he fails.

Frank and Aileen take possession of their New York home. Aileen discovers Frank's affair with Berenice Fleming, and, following a soul-scarring confrontation with him, attempts suicide. Frank prevents her from killing herself, but she feels that her life is finished. A new Governor is elected in Illinois, one more amenable to the Cowperwood interests. When in 1897 the Mears bill is passed, providing for the right of municipalities to grant long-term franchises, Governor Archer signs it into law. Now it is up to the Chicago City Council, largely in Cowperwood's employ, to determine whether his streetcar lines shall be given a monopoly for fifty years.

Cowperwood returns to Chicago and marshalls all his forces to assure that an ordinance providing for the franchise is passed. His rival financiers and the newspaper editors inimical to him join in the opposition, which now includes a new and powerful force, that of citizens' reform groups. In December 1898 the City Council meets to vote on the franchise ordinance. The galleries are packed with irate citizens, all of them aroused against the measure, many of them prepared to do violence to any alderman voting in favor of it. Thus confronted, even Aldermen Tiernan and Kerrigan are intimidated, and the Council turns down the ordinance.

The defeated Cowperwood decides that his wisest course of action will be to abandon his efforts in Chicago and attempt to realize his ambitions elsewhere. In this moment of dejection the sole ray of brightness is cast by Berenice Fleming, who comes from New York to offer herself to him. With her at his side Frank is confident that he will some day realize his dream of a truly gigantic and invincible financial career.

Judah Addison, Mrs. Judah (Ella) Addison, Corporal A. E. Archer, Edward Arneel, Timothy Arneel, Joel Avery, Millard Bailey, Hudson Baker, Corscaden Batjer, Mrs. Corscaden (Fredericka) Batjer, Arnold C. Benjamin, J J. Berg doll, Horton Biggers, Samuel Blackman, William Drake Bowdoin, Mrs. Brandon (Claudia Carlstadt), Lieutenant Lawrence Braxmar, Braxton, Bliss Bridge, Bradford Canda, Mrs. Bradford Canda, Claudia Carlstadt, Mrs. Ira George Carter (Hattie Starr), Rolfe Carter, Beales Chadsey, Aymar Cochrane, Florence Cochrane, Collard, Walter Rysam Cotton, Mrs. Walter Rysam Cotton, Lane Cross, Alfred B. Davis,

Nahum Dickensheets, Theresa Donovan, Patrick Dowling,
Clifford DuBois, Auguste Duelma, Kilmer Duelma, Duni-
way, Edstrom, Anthony Ewer, Fadette, Fishel, Berenice
Fleming, Mrs. John Alexander Fleming (Hattie Starr),
Jacob Gerecht, Patrick Gilgan, Gilleran, Colonel Nathaniel
Gillis, Rhees Grier, Forbes Gurney, Haatstaedt, Mrs. Haat-
staedt, Joseph Haeckelheimer, Augustus M. Haguenin,
Cecily Haguenin, Hosmer Hand, Mrs. Hosmer (Caroline
Barrett) Hand, Major Wickham Hedden, Nannie Hedden
(Hattie Starr), Jessie Belle Hinsdale, Stanislau Hoecksema,
Mrs. Stanislau Hoecksema, Dr. Hooper, Ella F. Hubby,
Mrs. Henry Huddleston, Phineas Hull, Walter Melville
Hyssop, Webster Israels, Mrs. Webster Israels, Hilda
Jewell, William Johnson, Jordan Jules, Solon Kaempfaert,
Edwin L. Kaffrath, Francis Kennedy, Patrick "Emerald
Pat"Kerrigan, Duane Kingsland, Gardner Knowles, Chrys-
tobel Lanman, Peter Laughlin, Mrs. Josephine Ledwell,
Toma Lewis, Taylor Lord, Mayor Walden H. Lucas, Mrs.
Walden H (Bessie) Lucas, Polk Lynde, General MacDonald,
Truman Leslie MacDonald, Oliver Marchbanks, Otto
Matjes, John J. McKenty, Kent Barrows McKibben, Anson
Merrill, Mrs. Anson (Nellie) Merrill, Terrence Mulgannon,
Antoinette Nowak, Dorothy Ormsby, Irma Ottley, Walter
Parker, Simon Pinski, Isadore Platow, Mrs. Isadore (Su-
setta Osborn) Platow, Stephanie Platow, Redmond Purdy,
Raymond Pyne, Alexander Rambaud, Mrs. Alexander Ram-
baud, Norman Schryhart, Bella Simms, Norrie Simms,
Henry De Soto Sippens, Watson Skeet, Onias C. Skinner,
Sutherland Sledd, Mrs. Sutherland Sledd, Mayor Chaffee
Thayer Sluss, Harold Sohlberg, Mrs. Harold (Rita Gree-
nough) Sohlberg, Senator John H. Southack, Benoni Stack-
pole, Hattie Starr (Mrs. Ira George Carter, Mrs. John
Alexander Fleming, Nannie Hedden), Burton Stimson,
Governor Swanson, Albert Thorsen, Michael "Smiling
Mike" Tiernan, Georgia Timberlake, Sylvester Toomey,
Davis Trask, Ethel Tuckerman, Ungerich, General Judson
P. Van Sickle, Videra, Isaac White, James Furnivale Wool-
sen.

A Trilogy of Desire, 1912-1947. See *The Financier, The Titan,* and *The
Stoic.*

"Typhoon," 1927.

The father and stepmother of Ida Zobel react against the blatant moral laxity of the present day by attempting to shield young Ida from its baleful influence. She is enrolled in a strict private school, and her every move is monitored. Meanwhile, beneath her restraints, Ida grows from ten to fourteen.

As she matures Ida finds the forbidden world ever more attractive and stuffed with promised joys. Even under the watchful eyes of her parents she finds it possible to have a moment or so for herself, time in which to admire the handsome soda clerk at the neighborhood drugstore. And she learns much vicariously through girl friends less regimented than she.

When Ida reaches sixteen, young Edward Hauptwanger, a coal-dealer's son, moves into her neighborhood. They are mutually attracted. Soon Edward is drifting into Zobel's paint store in order to be near the girl, and she is acutely conscious of his eager eyes and handsome features. When he learns of the restrictions placed upon Ida's activities, young Hauptwanger attempts to win her father's confidence by adopting a tone of complete frankness in speaking with him. Through his boldness and his apparent candor, he obtains permission to pay a formal call upon Ida twice a week.

Soon the Zobel family considers Edward to be a suitor. By degrees he is allowed further privileges, and with each new privilege his insistent nature forces new concessions from the infatuated Ida. At last, over her protests and best intentions, Edward succeeds in seducing her. This accomplished, his interest wanes. But Ida discovers that she is to have a child, and she insists upon holding Edward to the promise he had made: to marry her should a pregnancy result from their intimacy. Now, terrified of losing his freedom, the boy refuses to carry out his promise. Ida becomes desperate, particularly since her father notices Hauptwanger's absence and comments on it.

Ida considers the possibility of threatening Edward with a revolver which her father keeps in his store, but she decides against any such extreme act. However, her father begins to press her for some plausible explanation of the young man's absence. Why, after his long familiarity with Ida and the family, is he not ready to continue his courtship and perhaps marry her? Zobel tells Ida that she must marry Edward or publicly break off her relationship with him. In a deranged moment, during a struggle and without fully intending to, Ida shoots Edward with the pilfered gun. Ida finds herself instantly notorious when the press takes up the story of the love slaying and gives it out to the public in large headlines. On the day following the shooting, Edward dies, but not before he admits that he has wronged Ida. On this account she is not jailed but instead is placed in a home to await the birth of her child.

Ida is puzzled by many things, one of them being the apparent transformation of her parents from strict guardians of her virtue into understanding and compassionate sharers of her plight. Had she known beforehand that they might act in this manner, she would not have been afraid to approach them in sufficient time to avert the tragedy. In the home, her son Eric is born. She is then put on trial. Again the reporters close in upon her and sensational headlines result. However, by virtue of Edward's deathbed testimony, Ida is exonerated.

When the time arrives for Ida to leave the home and return to her parents, she cannot go on. She is too overcome with the loss of Edward, too bewildered over the meaning of all that has happened to her. Ida's own will to live has seeped away. She wanders into the lake which was the scene of many joyful meetings with Edward Hauptwanger and without any show of emotion drowns herself, thereby stimulating her final newspaper headline.

Lawrence Cross, Edward Hauptwanger, Jacob Hauptwanger, Elizabeth Hohstauffer, Etelka Shomel, Walter Stour, Lawrence Sullivan, Sven Volberg, Merton Webster, Ida Zobel, William Zobel, Mrs. William Zobel.

"The Victor," 1927.

A variety of sources cooperate in the effort to piece together an accurate portrait of the late financier, John Osterman. In an *Engineering Record* article, Osterman's chief engineer, G. A. Gridley, describes his late boss as a man of indomitable force, courage, and initiative: until his death he remained active and overflowed with bold ideas for new commercial ventures.

Others tell different stories about Osterman. C.B. Cummings, one-time secretary to the financier, describes the man's ruination of De Malquit, a broker. De Malquit had sold short on ten thousand shares of rubber stock—a trap set for him by Osterman, who then refused the man extra time in which to meet his debt. In this manner Osterman caused the broker's suicide and, subsequently, that of his invalid wife as well. Cummings relates also the case of Henry Greasadick.

Henry Greasadick located a giant oil field in the Southwest United States. But Osterman, by diverting the water which was essential to the Greasadick operation and by preventing the building of the railroad spur needed for hauling out the man's oil, caused Greasadick's ruination and death. Cummings tells also of the manner in which Osterman took over the C. C. and Q. L. Railroad by purchasing a few shares of stock and then initiating multiple stockholders' suits in order to frighten the company's investors and thereby drive down the price of its stock. This accomplished, Osterman was able to purchase the railroad line at a fraction of its true value.

Lingley's Magazine publishes a biographic study of J. H. Osterman. The article provides details concerning his difficult boyhood on the Kansas plains. Osterman's father had died when his son was a mere boy, eleven years old. The family farm fell victim to drought, then to a grasshopper plague, and in his dire poverty the maturing Osterman was so strongly influenced by religious maxims such as "an eye for an eye, a tooth for a tooth" that he ended as a ruthless industrial giant who asked no quarter and gave none.

During his last years on earth, John H. Osterman lived in his Fifth Avenue mansion. Often he reflected upon the hard times endured in his early years and upon the pleasures he derived from making a fortune once that goal had been identified. He regretted the many deaths he had caused—those of De Malquit, Greasadick, and others—but since he had not intended these he felt no actual blame for them. If anything, he thought that life itself must be held accountable; it was such a deceptive thing, and human beings so powerless ultimately. The pleasures that came from piling up a massive fortune did not endure for Osterman. He married the socially prominent Nadia, but was forced to balk at her overly obvious plan of persuading him to leave his great wealth to her wastrel sons.

Byington Briggs, a private legal adviser to Osterman, reminisces about the financier's last will. Briggs wrote it for him, and under its terms the widow, Nadia, and her two sons were to be granted the interest from a sizable lifetime trust. But the great bulk of the Osterman fortune was to go to an orphans' home. By an irony of life, before the draft of this final will could be polished and signed into legality, Osterman fell victim to a sudden attack of apoplexy. Life is wholly a matter of chance, Briggs reflects, and nothing more.

Byington Briggs, Esq., C. B. Cummings, De Malquit, Henry Greasadick, G. A. Gridley, Klippert, John H. Osterman, Mrs. John H. (Nadia Benda) Osterman.

"Victory," 1927. See "The Victor."

"The Wages of Sin," 1927. See "Typhoon."

"When the Old Century Was New," 1901.

In the New York of 1801, a young man, William Walton, takes the day off from his job in the counting house in order to attend to a number of pressing matters. All of these duties are highly important to Walton personally, although none of them has much import historically.

On the city's reservoir a test will be made this day of a new invention, a steamship. Below Wall Street the newly elected President of the United States, John Adams, tends his flower garden. At the wharf, John Jacob Astor discusses the potential of international commerce with other businessmen of the city. A house fire in William Street calls into play volunteers of one of the local bucket brigades.

Walton makes his way to Madame Kortright's mansion, a popular gathering place for the social crowd. Here all the talk and excitement centers on the house fire. Very little time is taken in speculating on the potential of the steamboat—considered by most to be a rather silly and even a dangerous notion. Even less attention is paid to a report of Benjamin Franklin's odd pronouncement that man before long will be harnessing the lightning in order to use its occult power.

After making his stop at Madame Kortright's, Walton calls upon his beloved, Beppie Cruger, whose chief concern is for the persistent encroachment of business houses upon her family's residential lot in Wall Street. The spread of businesses into residential areas is a disconcerting trend which threatens to drive the Crugers and other well-to-do residents to new homes further uptown.

William and Beppie go for a drive in a carriage, stopping at Maton's store, where a new exhibit of gems from France is on display. Beppie is attracted to a diamond ring, which William then purchases for her as an engagement present. As they leave the store they chance to pass Thomas Jefferson, who recognizes Walton and pays him the high compliment of addressing him by name. Somewhat ironically, Walton has not noticed Jefferson at all, being too preoccupied with the immediate excitement of his engagement to Beppie.

The young man—like the world he lives in—is caught up totally in things not of "historical" significance: youth, love, the beauty of nature. Like any other man, Walton has no means with which to gaze into the misty future and discern what his present moment may portend fr history.

John Adams, John Jacob Astor, Beppie Cruger, Jacob Cruger, Robert Goelet, Thomas Jefferson, Eulalie Kortright, Madame Kortright, William Van Rensalaer, William Walton.

"Will You Walk into My Parlor?", 1918.

Newspaperman Edward Gregory is on the trail of a really big story, the exposé of financial chicanery among local politicians, including the Mayor of his city. During the hot summer, while he amasses his data and prepares his story for publication close to election day, Gregory is warned that the politicians he is investigating will surely fight back. In order to protect himself he must avoid any act which can be made to appear illegal, immoral or unethical. Politicians in jeopardy will battle with any ammunition they can find.

Gregory goes to live at the Triton, a great hotel on Long Island, and here he feels relatively secure. Since reasons of health take Mrs. Gregory to the mountains, he is alone at Triton Hall. A fellow guest is Mrs. Skelton, a very friendly woman who continually engages him in converstation. For advice on his work and behavior, Gregory approaches an old friend, Frank Blount, an ex-newspaperman now a stockbroker. Blount suggests that Gregory protect himself by keeping a daily log of events sworn before a notary. Blount also, being relatively free, offers to come to the hotel on weekends and to serve as an eyewitness to Gregory's conduct.

Mrs. Skelton becomes solicitous, often inviting Edward Gregory to share her table at mealtime with her and her broker friends. Before long Mrs. Skelton is joined by the beautiful young Imogene Carle. The obvious possibility that the girl may be in the hire of his enemies arouses Gregory's suspicions. Nonetheless, trusting that his own wits will match whatever test they may encounter, he becomes acquainted with Imogene and often dines or goes joyriding with her and her group. By degrees he comes to believe Imogene innocent of any plot against him. Still, at Blount's urging he keeps his guard up and makes a contingent plan to persuade the girl to join his side of the political battle should he ever discover that his belief in her innocence is mistaken.

Mrs. Skelton and Imogene are joined by a tiny Jew, Mr. Diamondberg, presumably a clothing manufacturer, but a figure of some mystery to Gregory. They are joined also by a young Mr. Castleman, said to be heir to a fortune, who drives an immense blue automobile in which he takes Mrs. Skelton, Imogene, and Gregory for afternoon jaunts. Blount disapproves of these excursions and warns Gregory that he ought never to be alone with Imogene, since an automobile under another person's control can be used for any variety of "frames." Blount sees to it that he is Gregory's invariable guest on these auto rides.

Mrs. Skelton, when she and Gregory and Imogene take walks together, begins to develop a habit of needing to return to the hotel for some forgotten item. Gregory follows Blount's advice. He is careful not to proceed further with Imogene until the older woman returns. He begins to notice that whenever he drives with Mrs. Skelton another car follows. By the sound of its engine Gregory identifies the car as Castleman's. One night while Blount and Gregory are driving on the turnpike, they are sideswiped and nearly wrecked by Castleman's big auto. Castleman insists that the mishap is accidental, due to a faulty steering gear on his machine. But suspicions are raised nonetheless.

Blount discovers that Imogene Carle was once connected with the politicians whom Gregory expects to expose. Learning of this fact, Gregory confronts her with it; she denies the story, but when she learns the full extent of Gregory's information she confesses that she has agreed to repay past favors from them by attempting his seduction. She denies any knowledge of a plan to harm Gregory physically, and she throws herself on his mercy, pleading for sympathy.

Blount opposes any reconciliation; but because he is highly attracted to her, and because her story has the ring of plausibility to it, Gregory agrees not to abandon Imogene totally. Blount warns his friend not to compromise himself in any manner. Imogene confesses her own attraction to Gregory, and Blount suggests that Gregory should make certain that the girl falls deeply in love with him; he can then use this means to extract a written confession of her part in the plot against him.

One night Imogene lures Gregory to the hallway leading to her room. While he waits in the darkness she emerges in a disheveled state, clearly ready to scream for help and to accuse him of an assault. Gregory manages to escape, but he confronts the girl next morning and is told that she acted under duress. Her former accomplices, she says, waited in her room and forced her to rip her clothing. Imogene insists that, even so, she intended not to scream for aid, but to warn Gregory of the charade. He is dubious and puts her to a test. If she is sincere in her claim to being virtually a prisoner of malevolent forces, she will make a confession openly before a notary and will sign a written copy for the District Attorney. To Gregory's amazement, the girl acquiesces to the demand.

With this document in hand Gregory feels relatively secure, but he breaks with Imogene nevertheless. One day she telephones him and pleads for one last farewell meeting. He is suspicious, but he agrees to meet with her provided it is in some completely open and public spot. They meet in a café in the financial district. He tells her that he cannot afford to become involved in any activities that might in any manner tend to reflect either on his marriage or on his political investigation. Sadly, Imogene agrees to their separation.

Their lunch done, they leave the café. On the sidewalk outside, Imogene begs a goodbye kiss, and when Gregory bends to brush her cheek with his lips, she suddenly embraces him with passion. It is only when Gregory observes a pair of motion-picture cameras trained on him and running that he is fully aware of how thoroughly he has been duped after all. His months of effort in gathering evidence against the fraudulent politicians have been a total waste of time.

Frank Blount, Imogene Carle, Castleman, Diamondberg, Edward Gregory, Mrs. Edward (Emily) Gregory, Mrs. Skelton, Jack Swayne, Tilney.

CHARACTERS

Abdullah, Ibn. "Khat." A Moslem beggar of Hodeidah.

Abou. "The Prince Who Was a Thief." See Hussein, Prince.

Ackerman, Charles. *The Financier.* A poor and uneducated Negro who is sentenced at the same court session with Frank Cowperwood.

Adams, John. "When the Old Century Was New." The newly elected President of the United States.

Addison, Judah. *The Titan.* The President of the Lake City National Bank; he is Frank Cowperwood's first business ally in Chicago.

Addison, Mrs. Judah (Ella). *The Titan.* The wife of Judah Addison; she befriends Aileen Cowperwood.

Adele. "Old Rogaum and His Theresa." The keeper of a house of prostitution in the Rogaums' neighborhood.

Ahmed. "Khat." A carpet weaver in the city of Hodeidah.

Ajeeb. "The Prince Who Was a Thief." A cleaner of the market stalls in the bazaar of Hodeidah.

Albertson, Horace. *The Stoic.* A St. Louis railroad man approached by Frank Cowperwood as a possible replacement for him during his final illness.

Alden, Agnes. *An American Tragedy.* A sister of Roberta Alden, three years her junior.

Alden, Emily. *An American Tragedy.* A younger sister of Roberta Alden.

Alden, Ephraim. *An American Tragedy.* The grandfather of Roberta Alden.

Alden, Roberta. *An American Tragedy.* A worker in the Griffiths shirt and collar factory, Lycurgus, New York; she is the girlfriend of Clyde Griffiths, later his mistress. She drowns in Big Bittern Lake in the Adirondacks. At various times, Roberta passes under the aliases of Mrs. Clifford Golden, Mrs. Carl Graham, and Mrs. Ruth Howard.

Alden, Thomas. *An American Tragedy.* The younger brother of Roberta Alden.

Alden, Titus. *An American Tragedy.* The father of Roberta Alden; he is a farmer near Biltz, New York.

Alden, Mrs. Titus. *An American Tragedy.* The mother of Roberta Alden.

Alderson, Jonas. *The Financier.* A Pinkerton detective hired by Edward Malia Butler to spy on his daughter Aileen and Frank Cowperwood.

al-Din, Gazzar. "The Prince Who Was a Thief." A Moslem story-teller of Hodeidah. He attempts to make his day's expenses by telling the legend of Prince Hussein.

Almerting, "Connie." "Old Rogaum and His Theresa." A stationer's son, handsome but an idler; he courts Theresa Rogaum.

Amanda. *An American Tragedy.* The maid at the home of Samuel Griffiths in Lycurgus.

Ames, Robert. *Sister Carrie.* A cousin of Mrs. Vance; he is an electrical engineer, a brilliant man admired by Carrie Meeber.

Ammerman. *The Financier.* The secretary of the Board of the Philadelphia Stock Exchange. In the panic of 1873 it is his duty to announce business closures and suspensions.

Amundsen, Officer. "Sanctuary." A plainclothes policeman who patrols the region of New York surrounding 14th and K Streets; he tricks Madeleine and then arrests her for soliciting.

Anthony, Patricia. *An American Tragedy.* A member of the social set in Lycurgus, friend of Sondra Finchley.

Appleman. *An American Tragedy.* The operator of a dry-goods store in Biltz, New York; he at one time employed Roberta Alden.

Appleton, Stella. *The "Genius."* A girl friend of Eugene Witla in Alexandria, Illinois, when Eugene is seventeen.

Arbuthnot. "Chains." A business acquaintance of Upham Brainerd Garrison.

Arnold, Cal. "Phantom Gold." A farmer; he is a neighbor of the Queeders.

Arquin. *The "Genius."* An art dealer; he heads the Paris branch of New York's Kellner & Sons gallery.

Archer, Corporal A. E. *The Titan.* The Governor of Illinois during the later 1890s; he succeeds Governor Swanson and for a consideration of $500,000 signs the Mears Bill for Frank Cowperwood.

Arneel, Edward. *The Titan*. The son of Timothy Arneel; he succeeds his father upon the latter's death.

Arneel, Timothy. *The Titan*. A Chicago meat packer and millionaire; he is an enemy of Frank Cowperwood.

Arnold, David. *The Bulwark*. A psychology professor at Llewellyn College; Isobel Barnes is in love with him.

Astor, John Jacob. "When the Old Century Was New." The prominent New York businessman and social leader.

Attenbury, Legare. *An American Tragedy*. A lawyer and state senator; he chairs the Republican State Central Committee in New York and acts as counsel to the Finchley family of Lycurgus.

Atrisha. "The Prince Who Was a Thief." The mother of Princess Yanee.

Averard, Abel C. *The Bulwark*. The cashier of the Traders and Builders Bank in Philadelphia.

Avery, Joel. *The Titan*. An ex-state senator of Illinois in the employ of Frank Cowperwood during the early 1900s.

Axelrod, Maida. *An American Tragedy*. The girl friend of Hegglund, a bellboy at the Green-Davidson Hotel; she goes on the auto ride with Clyde Griffiths during which a young girl is killed.

Ayres, Mildred. "Married." An artistic friend of Duer Wilde.

Babbs, Sir Humphrey. *The Stoic*. An industrialist, appointed by Lord Stane and others to replace the dying Cowperwood as head of their London subway enterprise.

Baggott, Harley. *An American Tragedy*. One of the social group at Twelfth Lake; he visits the Thurstons' lodge and is with Clyde Griffiths when he first hears the weir-weir bird.

Bailey, Millard. *The Titan*. A tool of Frank Cowperwood; Cowperwood sends Stackpole to him in order to obtain a loan against his American Match stock.

Baker. *An American Tragedy*. An alias under which Clyde Griffiths makes calls to Roberta Alden through the Wilcox telephone at Biltz. See also Clyde Griffiths.

Baker, Freeborn K. *The Bulwark*. A Director of the Traders and Builders Bank in Philadelphia.

Baker, Hudson. *The Titan*. The President of the West Side Gas Company in Chicago; an enemy of Frank Cowperwood.

Baker, Mrs. Williston. *Jennie Gerhardt*. A Chicagoan who meets Jennie Gerhardt at the Hanson Fields'.

Bakht, Azad. "The Prince Who Was a Thief." A barber in the Moslem city of Hodeidah.

Ballogh, Jessica. "Chains." A Lexington, Kentucky, girl with whom Epham Garrison has first had an affair, then married, and later divorced.

Balsford. "A Story of Stories." The city editor of The *News;* he is Red Collins' boss on that paper.

Bamberger. *Sister Carrie.* A member of the Elks Lodge in Chicago; he is cast as Ray in the lodge's production of "Under the Gaslight" but is dropped before the play goes on stage.

Bangs, Frank. The *"Genius."* The superintendent of a furniture factory in Alexandria, Illinois; he marries Myrtle Witla.

Bangs, Mrs. Frank (Myrtle Witla). The *"Genius."* Eugene Witla's sister, a Christian Science enthusiast.

Barclay. "The Shadow." The author of *Heyday* and a lover of Beryl Dana Stoddard.

Barlow, Fred. "Free." A classmate of Wesley Haymaker at the Galliard School.

Barlow, Patience. *The Financier.* A Quaker girl; she is a childhood sweetheart of Frank Cowperwood in Philadelphia.

Barnes. *An American Tragedy.* The assistant to the Captain of bell-boys at the Green-Davidson Hotel in Kansas City.

Barnes, Cynthia. *The Bulwark.* A sister of Solon Barnes.

Barnes, Dorothea. *The Bulwark.* The second oldest daughter of Solon Barnes.

Barnes, Etta. *The Bulwark.* The youngest daughter of Solon Barnes; she breaks his heart by turning her back on Quakerism.

Barnes, Hannah. *The Bulwark.* The mother of Solon Barnes.

Barnes, Isobel. *The Bulwark.* The eldest daughter of Solon Barnes; an unhappy girl, she finds little solace in Quakerism.

Barnes, Orville. *The Bulwark.* The elder son of Solon Barnes; a good businessman but an indifferent Quaker.

Barnes, Mrs. Orville (Althea Stoddard). *The Bulwark.* The daughter of Isaac Stoddard, owner of the American Potteries of Dukla.

Barnes, Rufus. *The Bulwark.* An old Quaker, father of Solon Barnes.

Barnes, Solon. *The Bulwark.* The hero of the novel, a Quaker who attempts to partake in the commercial world and yet regulate his life according to Quaker precepts of simplicity.

Barnes, Mrs. Solon (Benecia Wallin). *The Bulwark.* The daughter of Justus Wallin; mother of Dorothea, Etta, Isobel, Orville, and Stewart Barnes.

Barnes, Stewart. *The Bulwark.* The son of Solon and Benecia Barnes; he commits suicide in jail because of shame at his implication in the death of Psyche Tanzer.

Barrett, Thomas. *An American Tragedy.* An Adirondack mountain guide who testifies at Clyde Griffiths' trial that he saw a man and a woman in a boat in Moon Cove at Big Bittern Lake.

Bates, Baker. *The "Genius."* A friend of Hudson Dula who helps Eugene Witla obtain employment with the Summerfield Advertising Agency.

Batjer, Corscaden. *The Titan.* A wealthy friend of Berenice Fleming, resident of Redding Hills, Long Island.

Batjer, Mrs. Corscaden (Fredericka). *The Titan.* A friend of Berenice Fleming; she invites Berenice to visit her Long Island estate, Hillcrest, during the period of Berenice's social acceptability.

Bauman. *Jennie Gerhardt.* A Columbus, Ohio, storekeeper who generously extends credit to Mrs. William Gerhardt.

Bavo, Dr. *An American Tragedy.* A physician of Coldwater, New York, who is invited to participate in the autopsy on Roberta Alden's body.

Beale, Dr. *Sister Carrie.* A physician who lives near the George Hurstwoods' in Chicago; he sees Hurstwood and Carrie Meeber riding on Washington Boulevard and inadvertently reveals it to Mrs. Hurstwood.

Beane, Roger. *An American Tragedy.* A rural postman who testifies at Clyde Griffiths' trial that he carried letters from Clyde to Roberta Alden at the Alden farm.

Beckwith, Judge. *The Financier.* A judge of the Pennsylvania Supreme Court, anti-Cowperwood in feeling, who hears Cowperwood's appeal for a new trial.

Becker, Everett. *An American Tragedy.* A newspaper reporter for the Bridgeburg *Republican* who covers the story of the discovery of Roberta Alden's body in Big Bittern lake.

Beemis, Dr. *An American Tragedy.* A Utica physician who is invited to participate in the autopsy on Roberta Alden's body.

Beers, Vincent. *The "Genius."* The instructor of Eugene Witla's class in illustration at the Chicago Art Institute.

Belknap, Alvin. *An American Tragedy.* A former New York state senator and Democratic assemblyman; he was a rival of Orville Mason for the office of District Attorney of Cataraqui County, New York, and is now a member of the firm hired by Samuel Griffiths to defend his nephew Clyde.

Benedict, Oren. *The "Genius."* The art director of the New York *World*; he hires Eugene Witla as a member of his staff.

Benigrace, Compton, Jr. *The Bulwark.* A schoolmate and later a business associate of Solon Barnes.

Benjamin, Arnold C. *The Titan.* The Director of the North Chicago City Railway Company, one of the group who sell out to Frank Cowperwood and thus facilitate his entry into Chicago street transit.

Bermudez, Mrs. *Sister Carrie.* A theatrical agent consulted by Carrie Meeber in her efforts to obtain stage employment.

Betts, Dr. *An American Tragedy.* A Bridgeburg physician invited to participate in the autopsy on Roberta Alden's body.

Bey, Ibrihim Abbas. *The Stoic.* An Arabian sheik, an acquaintance of Bruce Tollifer and Aileen Cowperwood in Paris at the turn of the century.

Bezenah, Jack. *The "Genius."* A journalist hired by Eugene Witla to assume the editorship of *Adventure Story* magazine while Eugene is highly placed at the United Magazine Corporation.

Bergdoll, J. J. *The Titan.* The President of the Hyde Park Gas and Fuel Company in Chicago, an underling of Frank Cowperwood.

Bhori. *"The Prince Who Was a Thief."* A tin-seller in the Moslem City of Hodeidah.

Biggen, R. T. *An American Tragedy.* An oil-station manager in Lycurgus, New York, who testifies at Clyde Griffiths' trial that he saw Clyde in the clothes worn by him on the trip to Big Bittern lake and later found buried near there.

Biggers, Horton. *The Titan.* The editor of the *Saturday Review*, a social-set weekly published in Chicago.

Bingham, Edward. *The Stoic.* A bond salesman in New York who provides Frank Cowperwood with confidential information regarding Bruce Tollifer.

Binns, Augustus. *"A Story of Stories."* A reporter on the *Star*; he is a rival of Red Collins.

Binwool, Martin. *Fine Furniture.* A logger in the logging camp at Red Ledge; a friend of Clem Broderson.

Binwool, Mrs. Martin. *Fine Furniture.* A logger's wife to whom Opal Broderson feels superior.

Blackman, Samuel. *The Titan.* The President of the South Side Gas Company in Chicago, an enemy of Frank Cowperwood.

Bland, Georges. "Married." A friend of Duer Wilde; he gives a dinner at the Plaza Hotel for Duer and sponsors his first piano recital in New York.

Blandish. *The Stoic.* A member of the London and County Bank.

Blount, Frank. "Will You Walk into My Parlor?" A newspaperman; he is a friend of Edward Gregory.

Blow, Judge. "Phantom Gold." A landholder in Taney; he discovers that the territory is rich in zinc.

Blue, Angela. *The "Genius."* See Witla, Mrs. Eugene (Angela Blue).

Blue, Benjamin. *The "Genius."* A brother of Angela Blue Witla.

Blue, David. *The "Genius."* A brother of Angela Blue Witla.

Blue, Jotham. *The "Genius."* A farmer of Blackwood, Wisconsin; he is the father of Angela Blue Witla.

Blue, Mrs. Jotham. *The "Genius."* The mother of Angela Blue Witla.

Blue, Marietta. *The "Genius."* The daughter of Mr. and Mrs. Jotham Blue; Eugene Witla is attracted to her, but she begs him to marry her sister, Angela, as he has promised to do.

Blue, Samuel. *The "Genius."* A brother of Angela Blue Witla.

Bode, Julian. *The Financier.* An ex-mayor of Philadelphia who becomes involved in shady business deals with Frank Cowperwood.

Bogart, Jack. *An American Tragedy.* A woodsman; he retrieves Clyde's camera from the area of Big Bittern lake in which Roberta Alden has drowned.

Bonhag, Walter. *The Financier.* A cell overseer in Eastern Penitentiary; he supervises Frank Cowperwood after the latter is transferred to Block Three; he trains Cowperwood in caning chairs.

Borchardt, Jacob. *The Financier.* The Mayor of Philadelphia in 1871 during Cowperwood's troubles there.

Borg, Sydney. "Married." A music critic on a New York newspaper.

Borodandaj, Guru. *The Stoic.* A Hindu teacher consulted by Berenice Fleming; during her tour of India he instructs her in yoga.

Bordaloue, Martha. *An American Tragedy.* A worker in Clyde's department at the Griffiths shirt and collar factory.

Bosvike, Lord. *The Stoic.* A guest of Lord Haddonfield at his home, Beriton Manor.

Bosvike, Lady. *The Stoic.* A friend of Lord Haddonfield; Cowperwood meets her at Haddonfield's country home and sees in her a potential means of entry into London society.

Botts, Lester. "Phantom Gold." A farmer who witnesses Bursay
    Queeder's agreement to sell his home to Crawford.
Bowdoin, William Drake. *The Titan.* A wealthy suitor of Berenice
    Fleming; he rejects her after rumors concerning her mother's
    past become current in New York.
Bowers, Stephen. "The Cruise of the 'Idlewild.'" A carpenter in the
    mill who is appointed able seaman aboard the mythical ship
    "Idlewild."
Boyle, Temple. *The "Genius."* An instructor at the Art Institute of
    Chicago; he is one of Eugene Witla's early teachers.
Bracebridge, Henry. *Jennie Gerhardt.* A wealthy Cleveland resident
    at whose home Jennie Gerhardt works as a maid.
Bracebridge, Mrs. Henry (Minnie). *Jennie Gerhardt.* A wealthy woman
    who is Jennie's first employer in Cleveland.
Brainerd, Mrs. Sidney (Marigold Shoemaker). *The Stoic.* A longtime
    friend of Bruce Tollifer from Bar Harbor and Long Island
    whom he meets once again while in Paris with Aileen Cow-
    perwood.
Braley, Mrs. *An American Tragedy.* An employee in the Griffiths
    shirt and collar factory in Lycurgus.
Brander, Hon. George Sylvester. *Jennie Gerhardt.* The junior senator
    from Ohio in 1880 who seduces Jennie but dies before he
    can marry her.
Brandon, Mrs. *The Titan.* See Carlstadt, Claudia.
Brandt, Flora. *An American Tragedy.* An employee in Clyde Griffiths'
    department of the shirt and collar factory in Lycurgus.
Braxmar, Lieutenant Lawrence. *The Titan.* A beau of Berenice Flem-
    ing; he comes from an old Carolina family. When the truth
    about Berenice's mother is revealed, he jilts her.
Braxton. *The Titan.* The editor of the Chicago *Globe,* an enemy of
    Cowperwood.
Bridge, Bliss. *The Titan.* A member of Chicago's amateur theatrical
    group, the Garrick Players.
Bridges, J. J. *The Financier.* A Philadelphia broker, member of the
    jury which deliberates the Frank Cowperwood embezzle-
    ment case.
Brierly. *Fine Furniture.* The topographical engineer for the Red
    Ledge logging company; his responsibilities include locating
    campsites for the logging crew.
Briggen, Tommy. *The Bulwark.* The son of a railroad section hand;
    he is a childhood friend of Solon Barnes.

Briggs, Byington, Esq. "The Victor." A legal advisor to the wealthy J. H. Osterman.

Briggs, Hortense. *An American Tragedy.* A shop girl at a Kansas City department store; Louise Ratterer introduces her to Clyde Griffiths, and he rapidly becomes infatuated with her.

Briggs, Letitia. *The Bulwark.* The headmistress of a private school for the children of Friends at Red Kiln, Pennsylvania.

Briscoe, Arnold. *The Bulwark.* The father of Walter Briscoe; an upstanding member of the Quaker community in Philadelphia.

Briscoe, Walter. *The Bulwark.* A trusted Quaker youth who shakes Solon Barnes' faith by embezzling from the Traders and Builders Bank in Philadelphia.

Bristol, Oliver. *The Stoic.* A youthful member of Frank Cowperwood's legal department.

Bristol, Shorty. *An American Tragedy.* An inmate of Auburn Prison in New York State.

Bristow, Arthur. "The Second Choice." Shirley's handsome and attractive but deceiving boy friend; he induces her to jilt her beau, Barton Williams, and then he abandons her.

Broderson, Clem. *Fine Furniture.* An engine man working for a logging company in Red Ledge; he is a simple man who cannot understand or effectively deal with his wife's pretensions.

Broderson, Mrs. Clem (Opal). *Fine Furniture.* A waitress who marries Clem Broderson as a means of gaining social status; she offends the entire logging camp at Red Ledge by her pretensions.

Brookhart, Darrah *An American Tragedy.* A legal counsel for Samuel Griffiths in Lycurgus.

Brookshaw. *An American Tragedy.* A Utica family who own a lake cottage in the Adirondack mountains.

Browne, Gaither. "Chains." A Chicagoan who once was in love with Idelle; because he believed she might leave him, he attempted to kill her and himself by means of an automobile accident.

Bruge, Victor. *The Bulwark.* A classmate of Stewart Barnes at Franklin Hall School; he administers the tranquilizing drug which inadvertently causes the death of Psyche Tanzer.

Bruning, Bud. *An American Tragedy.* A youth who meets Clyde Griffiths as he is escaping from the Big Bittern area and who later testifies to that effect at his trial.

Burgess, Benjamin C. *The "Genius."* The father-in-law of Sylvia Witla Burgess; he is the editor and proprietor of the Alexandria, Illinois, *Morning Appeal*.

Burgess, Henry. *The "Genius."* The son of Benjamin Burgess; he marries Sylvia Witla.

Burgess, Mrs. Henry (Sylvia Witla). *The "Genius."* The sister of Eugene Witla.

Burleigh, Burton. *An American Tragedy.* A legal assistant in the office of district attorney Orville Mason.

Burt, Alys. *The Bulwark.* A student at Vassar College; she is a friend of Rhoda Wallin.

Butler, Aileen. *The Financier; The Titan; The Stoic.* See Cowperwood, Mrs. Frank Algernon (Aileen Butler).

Butler, Callum. *The Financier.* The second son of Edward Butler; he is a clerk in the Philadelphia City Water Department.

Butler, Edward Malia. *The Financier.* A self-made man, a wealthy contracter of sewers, water mains, and streets in Philadelphia; he is instrumental in the conviction of Frank Cowperwood for embezzlement of municipal funds. In hiring a detective to investigate his daughter's reported liaison with Frank Cowperwood, he assumes the alias of Scanlon.

Butler, Mrs. Edward Malia. *The Financier.* The robust, if illiterate, mother of Aileen Butler.

Butler, Norah. *The Financier.* The second daughter of Edward Butler, his youngest child.

Butler, Owen. *The Financier.* The eldest son of Edward Butler; he is a member of the Pennsylvania state legislature.

Cadrigan, Beryl. *The Bulwark.* The daughter of close friends of the Segar Wallinses; they live in New Brunswick, New Jersey.

Calligan, Katharine. *The Financier.* A widowed dressmaker patronized by Aileen Butler.

Calligan, Mamie. *The Financier.* A classmate of Aileen Butler at St. Agatha's School; in the event she must leave home as a result of her liaison with Cowperwood, Aileen plans to live with Mamie and her dressmaker mother.

Calthorpe. *The Stoic.* The Chairman of the Traffic Electrical Company in London, which holds a subway franchise important to Frank Cowperwood.

Camden, Dr. *The Stoic.* A physician on board the *S. S. Empress* who treats Frank Cowperwood en route to New York when he is stricken with Bright's disease.

Canda, Bradford. *The Titan.* A Chicago jeweler.

Canda, Mrs. Bradford. *The Titan.* She is one of the few Chicagoans who are friendly to Aileen Cowperwood.

Cargill. *Sister Carrie.* The owner of the Cargill stable in Chicago, who accompanies George Hurstwood to the Elks' production of "Under the Gaslight"; they meet again in New York when Hurstwood is on his decline.

Carle, Imogene. "Will You Walk into My Parlor?" A Cincinnati girl who attempts to seduce newspaperman Edward Gregory in order to end his political investigations.

Carlstadt, Claudia. *The Titan.* A beautiful young woman who, in the guise of Mrs. Brandon, is hired by Frank Cowperwood to seduce Mayor Chaffee Thayer Sluss of Chicago and thereby render him susceptible to blackmail.

Carr, Buckner. *The Stoic.* The head butler employed in Frank Cowperwood's New York mansion.

Carter, Mrs. Ira George. *The Titan; The Stoic.* The mother of Berenice Fleming; born Nannie Hedden; under the name of Hattie Starr, she runs a brothel in Louisville, Kentucky, where Frank Cowperwood first encounters her daughter's photograph; she is known also as Mrs. John Alexander Fleming.

Carter, Rolfe. *The Titan; The Stoic.* The son of Mrs. Ira George Carter (Hattie Starr) and brother of Berenice Fleming; Frank Cowperwood gives him employment as secretary to one of his business underlings.

Castleman. "Will You Walk into My Parlor?" A wealthy friend of Imogene Carle and Mrs. Skelton.

Catchuman. *An American Tragedy.* An associate of Darrah Brookhart who, after Clyde Griffiths' arrest, is sent by his uncle Samuel to Bridgeburg to interrogate him and arrange for his defense.

Cavanaugh, Thomas. "St. Columba and the River." McGlathery's foreman on the work gang which is building the tunnel under the Hudson River.

Chadsey, Beales. *The Titan.* A Louisville native who while drunk encounters Berenice Fleming's mother in the Waldorf Astoria Hotel and unmasks her before Lieutenant Braxmar.

Chance, Bryon. *The Stoic.* A member of the London legal firm of

Rider, Bullock, Johnson, and Chance; the firm works with Cowperwood in his attempt to gain control of London subways.

Channing, Christina. *The "Genius."* A soloist with the New York Symphony Orchestra with whom Eugene Witla has a love affair.

Chapin, Elia. *The Financier.* A Quaker cell overseer in Eastern Penitentiary in charge of the "manners squad"; he instructs Frank Cowperwood in prison regulations.

Charles, Anatole. *The "Genius."* The manager of the New York branch of Kellner and Son Gallery who gives Eugene Witla his first one-man show.

Chudi. "The Prince Who Was a Thief." A baker in the Moslem city of Hodeidah.

Citron, Jig. *Fine Furniture.* A tool dresser in the logging camp at Red Ledge; he is a friend of Clem Broderson.

Citron, Mrs. Jig. *Fine Furniture.* A tool-dresser's wife; Opal Broderson feels that Mrs. Citron is beneath her.

Citron, Ella. *Fine Furniture.* The nine-year-old daughter of Jig and Mrs. Citron.

Clifford, Lady. *The Stoic.* A guest, with Frank Cowperwood and Berenice Fleming, on Lord Stane's yacht, *Ida.*

Cochrane, Aymar. *The Titan.* The director of the West Chicago Street Railway Company; he is the father of Florence Cochrane.

Cochrane, Florence. *The Titan.* One of Frank Cowperwood's mistresses in Chicago.

Coggleshall. *The Bulwark.* A youthful boy friend of Benecia Wallin.

Cole, Raphael. *The Stoic.* A retired New York banker whom Frank Cowperwood hopes to interest in his London venture since he profited by investing in Cowperwood's Chicago properties.

Colfax, Hiram C. *The "Genius."* A wealthy publisher who controls the Swinton-Scudder-Davis Company; he employs Eugene Witla and places him in charge of his corporation.

Colfax, Mrs. Hiram C. (Cecile). *The "Genius."* The wife of the publisher.

Collard. *The Titan.* A Chicago hotel man who owns an outstanding art collection.

Collins, David "Red." "A Story of Stories." See Kolinsky, David.

Collins, Tom. *The Financier.* A Philadelphian who assumes the role
of Edward Malia Butler's political heir.

Colvay, Lord. *The Stoic.* One of the twelve directors of the Metropolitan subway line in London.

Comiskey, Patrick Gavin. *The Financier.* A Philadelphia City Councilman; he is a silent partner in Edward Butler's contracts
for the hauling of city slops.

Constantia, Sister. *The Financier.* The Mother Superior at St.
Agatha's, Aileen Butler's convent school; when Edward
Butler plans to send Aileen abroad, he has Sister Constantia
in mind for her chaperone.

Cooke, Jay. *The Financier.* The famous Philadelphia financier; he
is said to be a rising personality in banking and a friend to
Frank Cowperwood.

Coombs, Joseph. *The Bulwark.* A farm hand hired by Solon Barnes.

Cotton, Walter Rysam. *The Titan.* A wholesale coffee broker in
Chicago.

Cotton, Mrs. Walter Rysam. *The Titan.* A Chicago society woman
who remains friendly with the Cowperwoods despite their
social repudiation by most of the city's powerful families.

Coulstone, J. "Chains." A Pittsburgh manufacturer who has had
a love affair with Idelle.

Court, Sutro. *The Bulwark.* A friend of the Segar Wallinses.

Courtright, C. B. *The Stoic.* The Governor of Arkansas in the 1900-
era; he is Cowperwood's fellow passenger aboard the *Kaiser
Wilhelm der Grosse.*

Cowperwood, Anna Adelaide. *The Financier.* The sister of Frank
Algernon Cowperwood.

Cowperwood, Edward. *The Financier.* A younger brother of Frank
Algernon Cowperwood.

Cowperwood, Frank Algernon. *The Financier; The Titan; The Stoic.*
The hero of the Financier trilogy, who begins his business
career in Philadelphia, continues it in New York, and concludes it in London. While he is meeting Aileen Butler clandestinely in *The Financier*, he uses the alias of Montague, and
in *The Stoic* he temporarily passes under the alias of Mr.
Dickson while vacationing in Norway with Berenice Fleming.

Cowperwood, Mrs. Frank Algernon (Aileen Butler). *The Financier;
The Titan; The Stoic.* The second Mrs. Cowperwood, married
to the financier following his divorce from Lillian Semple
Cowperwood in the 1880-era. In order to meet Cowperwood

clandestinely, she uses the alias of Mrs. Montague.

Cowperwood, Mrs. Frank Algernon (Lilliam Semple). *The Financier; The Titan; The Stoic.* The first Mrs. Cowperwood and the mother of Frank's two children, Lillian and Frank, Jr. In *The Stoic* she is, unaccountably, referred to as Mrs. Anna Wheeler.

Cowperwood, Frank Algernon, Jr. *The Financier; The Stoic.* The only son of the great financier.

Cowperwood, Henry Worthington. *The Financier.* The father of Frank Algernon Cowperwood; he is a prominent Philadelphia banker.

Cowperwood, Mrs. Henry Worthington (Nancy Arabella Davis). *The Financier.* The mother of Frank Algernon Cowperwood.

Cowperwood, Lillian. *The Financier; The Stoic.* Frank Algernon Cowperwood's only daughter; in *The Stoic* she is represented as being married and is referred to, somewhat unaccountably, as Mrs. *Anna* Templeton.

Craig, Mrs. *Jennie Gerhardt.* A neighbor of Jennie Gerhardt in the Hyde Park area of Chicago.

Crane, Dr. *An American Tragedy.* A physician of the Biltz area who treats the Titus Alden family.

Cranston. *An American Tragedy.* A Lycurgus, New York, manufacturer, owner of the Cranston Wickwire Company; Clyde Griffith stays at the Cranston Lodge on Twelfth Lake in the Adirondacks.

Cranston, Bertine. *An American Tragedy.* The daughter of the Lycurgus manufacturer, a friend of the Samuel Griffiths family.

Cranston, Grant. *An American Tragedy.* A close friend of Gilbert Griffiths: he is a member of the younger social set in the Adirondack lake region.

Crawford. "Phantom Gold." A prospector for zinc who is interested in purchasing the Queeder farm for its minerals.

Cross, Lane. *The Titan.* A portrait painter who helps to stage performances given by the Garrick Players in Chicago; he is Stephanie Platow's second lover.

Cross, Lawrence. "Typhoon." A friend of Ida Zobel.

Crowell, Sophia. *The Bulwark.* A maid-companion to Hester Wallin; she serves her mistress for thirty years.

Cruger, Jacob. "When the Old Century Was New." A wealthy merchant of New York in 1801; he is the father of Beppie Cruger.

Cruger, Beppie. "When the Old Century Was New." A belle of old New York; the daughter of Jacob Cruger.

Cullen. "The Cruise of the 'Idlewild.'" A millwright in the shop which is the setting for the story.

Cummings, C. B. "The Victor." A secretary to the wealthy J. H. Osterman.

Cunningham, William H. *The Stoic.* A New York court officer; after Frank Cowperwood's death, he is appointed as Receiver of the financier's property.

Cuppy, Mrs. *An American Tragedy.* Clyde Griffiths' first landlady in Lycurgus, New York.

Cuthbert. *The Stoic.* A New York art expert to whom Frank Cowperwood entrusts the care of his collection during his absence from the city.

Cutronc, Pasquale. *An American Tragedy.* An inmate on Death Row in Auburn Prison; he is executed during Clyde Griffiths' time at Auburn.

Dabe, Luther. *The Bulwark.* A friend of the Segar Wallinses.

Dale, Mrs. Emily. *The "Genius."* A widow of thirty-eight, mother of Suzanne Dale; she writes for the United Magazine Corporation headed by Eugene Witla.

Dale, Kinroy. *The "Genius."* Suzanne's brother; he creates the plan to spirit her to Canada far from Eugene.

Dale, Quincy. *An American Tragedy.* A railroad conductor on the run between Fonda and Utica, New York; he testifies at Clyde Griffiths' trial that he saw Clyde and Roberta on the train shortly before the girl's death.

Dale, Suzanne. *The "Genius."* The beautiful teen-age daughter of Mrs. Emily Dale; Eugene Witla becomes enamored of her and ruins his journalistic career for her sake.

Dalrymple. *The Financier.* A grocer in Philadelphia; he purchases the soap which thirteen-year-old Frank Cowperwood has obtained at an auction.

Dana, Alice. "The Shadow." The sister of Beryl Dana Stoddard.

Davi, Adam. *The Financier.* The First Vice President of the Third National Bank in Philadelphia; he works under Henry Worthington Cowperwood.

David, Father. *The Financier.* A priest at St. Timothy's, the home parish of the Edward Butler family.

Davidson. "The Hand." An adventurous gold miner who kills his partner, Mersereau, and believes himself to be haunted by the dead man's spirit.

Davies, Elmer. "Nigger Jeff." A newspaper reporter assigned to cover the story of the purported rape of Ada Whitaker for which Jeff Ingalls is lynched.

Davis, Alfred B. *The Titan.* A Chicago Councilman and manufacturer of willow and rattan furniture; he cooperates with Frank Cowperwood in obtaining gas franchises in the Hyde Park area.

Davis, Mrs. *The Financier.* The keeper of a house of assignation in South Tenth Street, Philadelphia, where Frank Cowperwood meets with Aileen Butler.

Davis, Mrs. *Jennie Gerhardt.* Jennie's neighbor in Sandwood.

Davis, Mrs. Marie. "Convention." The mistress of Wallace Steele.

Davis, Seneca. *The Financier.* The maternal uncle of Frank Algernon Cowperwood; he owns a lucrative plantation in Cuba.

Davis, Mrs. Seneca. *The Financier.* The aunt of Frank Algernon Cowperwood.

Davison, W. C. *The Financier.* The President of the Girard National Bank in Philadelphia; he testifies at Frank Cowperwood's trial for embezzlement.

Day, Charles. *The Stoic.* A lawyer engaged by Aileen Butler Cowperwood to represent her in the litigation concerning Frank Cowperwood's estate.

Deegan, Timothy. *The "Genius."* The Irish foreman of a gang of Italian railroad workers near Riverwood and Speonk, New York; during his recuperation from neurasthenia, Eugene Witla joins this crew as a form of occupational therapy.

de Fremmery, Ethel. *The Bulwark.* A girl friend of Victor Bruge, Stewart Barnes' schoolmate.

De Gaud, George. "Free." The father-in-law of Wesley Haymaker.

De Gaud, Mrs. George. "Free." The mother-in-law of Wesley Haymaker.

De Gaud, Irma. "Free." See Haymaker, Mrs. Wesley (Irma De Gaud).

Delafield. *The Stoic.* The secretary and treasurer of the Traffic Electrical Company in London.

Delahanty, Officer. "Old Rogaum and His Theresa." A policeman in the Rogaums' district of New York City.

De Malquit. "The Victor." A business competitor of J. H. Osterman who commits suicide after being ruined by him.

Dempsey, Malachi. *The "Genius."* A plane driver on the railroad crew which Eugene Witla joins near Riverwood, New York.

Denton. *The Stoic.* An employee of Frank Cowperwood; he acts as secretary to Henry De Sota Sippens in London; together they work in Cowperwood's interest.

De Sale, Miss. *The "Genius."* A nurse who treats Angela Blue Witla during her childbirth.

Desenas, Mrs. *The "Genius."* The landlady of Eugene and Angela Witla while they are living in Riverwood, New York.

Desmas, Michael. *The Financier.* The Warden of Eastern Penitentiary in Philadelphia; at the request of politician Terrence Relihan, he takes a personal interest in the welfare of Frank Cowperwood while the financier is incarcerated.

Dexter, Russell. *The "Genius."* An artist who leases his studio in Greenwich Village to Eugene and Angela Witla following their marriage.

Diamondberg. *"Will You Walk into My Parlor?"* A Jewish friend of Mrs. Skelton at the Triton Hotel on Long Island.

Dickensheets, Hon. Nahum. *The Titan.* A judge on the Illinois State Court of Appeals; he is suborned by Frank Cowperwood.

Dickerman, Rita. *An American Tragedy.* A girl friend of Walter Dillard, one of Clyde Griffiths' first acquaintances in Lycurgus.

Dickson. *The Stoic.* See Cowperwood, Frank Algernon.

Dighton, Sir Hudspeth. *The Stoic.* A Director of the District subway line in London.

Dillard, Walter. *An American Tragedy.* The son of a dry-goods store proprietor in Fonda, New York; he is a fellow boarder with Clyde Griffiths at Mrs. Cuppy's in Lycurgus

Dodge, Berry. *Jennie Gerhardt.* A millionaire dry-goods manufacturer; he is a long-time friend of Lester Kane.

Dodge. *"The Lost Phoebe."* A farmer, neighbor to the Henry Reifsneiders.

Dodge, Simeon. *An American Tragedy.* A woodsman and diver who helps to take Roberta Alden's body from Big Bittern lake, he finds the camera dropped in the lake by Clyde Griffiths.

Dodson. *The "Genius."* The manager of the printing department at United Magazine Corporation; he works with Eugene Witla.

Dolan. *The Stoic.* A Philadelphian whom Frank Cowperwood names as one of the five executors of his last will.

Donahue, J. L. *The Stoic.* An auctioneer who presides at the sale of

Frank Cowperwood's New York properties.

Donahue, Larry. *An American Tragedy.* An inmate of Auburn Prison during Clyde Griffiths' incarceration.

Donahue, Mrs. Rutger. *An American Tragedy.* A woman who at Clyde Griffiths' trial testifies that she was at Moon Cove, Big Bittern lake, and heard a woman scream in pain at the time that Clyde and Roberta Alden were boating there.

Donovan, Theresa. *The Titan.* A leading couturière in Chicago, partonized by Aileen Cowperwood.

Doody, Jerry. *Fine Furniture.* Woodchopper to a donkey engine in the logging camp at Red Ledge; he is a friend of Clem Broderson.

Doody, Mrs. *Fine Furniture.* The mother of Jerry Doody; she keeps house for him in Red Ledge.

Dorsey, Dr. "Chains." A friend of Upham Garrison who treats Idelle in the hospital after her automobile accident.

Dowling, Patrick. *The Titan.* A Chicago alderman, subordinate in politics to John J. McKenty.

Doyle, Eddie. *An American Tragedy.* One of Clyde Griffiths' fellow bellhops at the Green-Davidson Hotel in Kansas City.

Drake, Stanford. *The Stoic.* A powerful American financier who in 1902 challenges Frank Cowperwood for control of London subways but loses to him.

Drexel, Francis. *The Financier.* The Philadelphia banker; Cowperwood appeals to him for help in his financial difficulties in 1871.

Drouet, Charles H. *Sister Carrie.* A salesman for the Bartlett, Caryoe and Company manufacturing concern who befriends Carrie Meeber as she enters Chicago; later Drouet takes her as his mistress.

Du Bois, Clifford. *The Titan.* The managing editor of the Chicago *Inquirer*, inimical to Frank Cowperwood.

Duelma, Kilmer. *The Titan.* The son of a millionaire banker; he is a friend of the Batjers of Long Island, who consider him to be a potential suitor for Berenice Fleming.

Duff, Margaret. *The "Genius."* A worker in a Chicago laundry who initiates Eugene Witla sexually soon after he comes to the city.

Dula, Hudson. *The "Genius."* The art director of *Truth*; he befriends Eugene Witla.

Duncan, John "Jack." *The "Genius."* A member of the railroad crew which Eugene Witla joins in Riverwood, New York.

Duniway. *The Titan.* A Chicago councilman and druggist; he cooperates with Frank Cowperwood in setting up a gas company in Lake View.

Eberling. *The Bulwark.* A bank examiner; he investigates the Traders
and Builders Bank in Philadelphia.

Edmunds, William. *The Stoic.* A director of the Railway Equipment
and Construction Company of London.

Edstrom. *The Titan.* The political leader of the Swedes in Chicago.

el-Din, Zad. "The Prince Who Was a Thief." A seller of piece goods
in the city of Hodeidah.

Elfridge, Mrs. "Free." The caretaker of the Haymaker apartment.

Ellison, Judge. *The Bulwark.* A friend of the Segar Wallinses.

Ellsworth, Wilton. *The Financier.* A Philadelphia architect who re-
models the Semple home for the Frank Cowperwoods after
their marriage; later he designs the Cowperwood home on
Girard Avenue.

Ellwanger, Dr. *Jennie Gerhardt.* A Columbus, Ohio, physician who
assists Jennie in her pregnancy and childbirth.

Emily. "Old Rogaum and His Theresa." A prostitute who attempts
suicide in the Rogaums' district of New York.

Emory, Dr. *Jennie Gerhardt.* A Chicago physician who treats Jennie's
daughter, Vesta, in her final illness.

Ermi. "McEwen of the Shining Slave Makers." A Lucidi ant.

Etheridge, Mrs. Leah. *The Bulwark.* A Quaker woman who asks
for prayers for her son William.

Ettinge, Lord. *The Stoic.* A Britisher prominent in the railway and
shipping fields; he is a guest of Lord Haddonfield at Beriton.

Ettinge, Lady. *The Stoic.* A guest of Lord Haddonfield at Beriton at
the same time that Cowperwood visits there.

Eugster, William. *The Financier.* A felon sentenced for breaking and
entering at the same court session as Frank Cowperwood,
1872.

Evans, Jack. *An American Tragedy.* The proprietor of the hotel at
Grass Lake, New York, where Clyde Griffiths registers as
Carl Graham.

Evans, Mrs. *The Stoic.* A housekeeper in service to Berenice Fleming
at her Pryor's Cove home on the Thames River.

Ewer, Anthony. *The Titan.* A director of the North Chicago City
Railway Company; he is a member of the group who sell
out to Frank Cowperwood.

Fadette. *The Titan.* A maid in service to Aileen Cowperwood in Chicago.

Feliss, Opal. *An American Tragedy.* An employee at the Cranston Wickwire factory in Lycurgus; she lives at the Newtons' with Roberta Alden.

Feruz. "The Prince Who Was a Thief." A water carrier in the Moslem city of Hodeidah.

Fessler, Robert. *An American Tragedy.* The secretary to the Governor of New York at the time he is appealed to in the attempt to save Clyde Griffiths' life.

Field, Mrs. Hanson. *Jennie Gerhardt.* A close neighbor to Jennie when she lives in Hyde Park, Illinois.

Filson, Miss. "Free." The nurse who attends Mrs. Haymaker in her final illness.

Finch, Miriam. *The "Genius."* A sculptress whom Eugene Witla meets through Richard Wheeler.

Finchley, Sondra. *An American Tragedy.* A wealthy girl of Lycurgus, New York, who professes to love Clyde Griffiths and whom Clyde supposes to be his means of entry into wealth and social status.

Fishel. *The Titan.* A banker of the firm of Fishel, Stone, and Symons who backs Frank Cowperwood and, in company with Haekelheimer, brings the rival Chicago streetcar lines to Cowperwood in 1897, dependent on Cowperwood's winning franchises which will be good for fifty years.

Fitler, Doris. *The Financier.* A childhood sweetheart of Frank Algernon Cowperwood.

Fitzpatrick, Nellie. "Sanctuary." See Kinsella, Madeleine.

Fleming, Berenice. *The Titan; The Stoic.* The last and most important mistress of Frank Algernon Cowperwood; he attempts to groom her for social conquest, but when her mother's lurid past is exposed, that dream is smashed; while following Cowperwood in his travels she uses the name Kathryn Trent.

Fleming, Mrs. John Alexander. *The Titan; The Stoic.* See Carter, Mrs. Ira George.

Fornes, Harry. *The "Genius."* A blacksmith with the railroad crew which Eugene Witla joins in Riverwood, New York.

Forster, Rufus. *An American Tragedy.* A surveyor for the county, who testifies at Clyde Griffiths' trial.

Frank. "The Old Neighborhood." The son of the narrator; he dies of influenza at an early age.

Fraser, Benjamin. *The Financier.* A mining expert who is selected as a member of the Frank Cowperwood jury in 1871.

Frazer, Joseph. *An American Tragedy.* A salesman who testifies at Clyde Griffiths' trial that Clyde purchased from him the camera and tripod later found on the site of Roberta Alden's death.

Frazer, Miss. *The Bulwark.* A teacher at the Oakwold School, to which Friends traditionally send their children.

Fredericks. *The "Genius."* A partner in the Kalvin Publishing Company for which Eugene Witla works for a time.

Frederickson. *The Stoic.* A valet in service to Frank Algernon Cowperwood at the turn of the century.

Frères, Pottle. *The "Genius."* A New York art dealer who undertakes to sell Eugene Witla's paintings for him.

Gadge, Alfred. *The Bulwark.* An assistant director at the Traders and Builders Bank in Philadelphia.

Gair, Pet. *The Bulwark.* A friend of Rhoda and Segar Wallin.

Garrison, Upham Brainerd. "Chains." The hero of the story; his fascination with his wife, Idelle, endures beyond all her infidelities and despite all his resolutions to abandon her.

Garrison, Mrs. Upham Brainerd (Idelle). "Chains." A life-loving and impetuous girl who follows her every inclination, confident that her husband will remain true to her.

Gault, Reverend Francis. *An American Tragedy.* An officer in the Salvation Army of Auburn, New York.

Gault, Mrs. Francis. *An American Tragedy.* A Salvationist; Elvira Griffiths is with Mrs. Gault and her husband at the time that Clyde Griffiths dies in the electric chair for the murder of Roberta Alden.

Genderman. *The Financier.* A Philadelphia grain dealer.

George. "Chains." The Negro servant of Upham Brainerd Garrison.

Gerald, Mrs. Malcolm (Letty Pace). *Jennie Gerhardt.* See Kane, Mrs. Lester (Letty Pace Gerald).

Gerhardt, Genevieve "Jennie." *Jennie Gerhardt.* The heroine of the novel, known for her gentle ways and giving nature. In her later life Jennie assumes the alias of Mrs. J. G. Stover.

Gerhardt, George. *Jennie Gerhardt.* Jennie's younger brother.

Gerhardt, Martha. *Jennie Gerhardt.* Jennie's younger sister.

Gerhardt, Veronica. *Jennie Gerhardt.* See Sheridan, Mrs. Albert (Veronica Gerhardt).

Gerhardt, Sebastian "Bass." *Jennie Gerhardt.* Jennie's oldest brother;

it is on his account that she begs from Senator Brander.

Gerhardt, Wilhelmina Vesta. *Jennie Gerhardt.* Jennie's illegitimate daughter by Senator Brander; in Chicago she passes under the name of Vesta Stover.

Gerhardt, William. *Jennie Gerhardt.* Jennie's rigidly Lutheran father; he is a glass blower by trade.

Gerhardt, Mrs. William. *Jennie Gerhardt.* Jennie's mother, a compassionate German woman.

Gerhardt, William, Jr. *Jennie Gerhardt.* Jennie's younger brother.

Gettler, Bert. *An American Tragedy.* A boy friend of Hortense Briggs and a romantic rival of Clyde Griffiths.

Gildus, Betty. "Chains." A friend of Idelle Garrison.

Giles, Anthony. "Phantom Gold." A rascally lawyer of Taney who participates in the sale of the Queeder farm.

Gilgan, Patrick. *The Titan.* A Chicago politician and saloonkeeper who is chosen by Hosmer Hand to run for state senator on the Republican ticket against McKenty and the Frank Cowperwood interests.

Gilleran, Alderman. *The Titan.* A Chicago politician who leads the anti-Cowperwood forces in the City Council.

Gilligan, "Red." *The Financier.* A young Philadelphia rowdy, boyhood friend of Frank Cowperwood.

Gillis, Colonel Nathaniel. *The Titan.* A wealthy horseman and inventor of Louisville, Kentucky, who introduces Frank Cowperwood to Hattie Starr and her establishment.

Gilman, Georgette. *The Bulwark.* A girl friend of Stewart Barnes' schoolmate Victor Bruge.

Gilpin, Mrs. *An American Tragedy.* A Lycurgus landlady; after Roberta Alden leaves the Newtons' she takes a room at Mrs. Gilpin's house.

Gilpin, Stella. *An American Tragedy.* Mrs. Gilpin's daughter, a friend of Roberta Alden; she testifies at Clyde Griffiths' trial.

Givens, Alassandra. *The Stoic.* A New York society girl, shipmate of the Frank Cowperwoods aboard the *Kaiser Wilhelm der Grosse* in the 1900-era.

Glassberg, Simon. *The Financier.* A Philadelphia clothier selected to serve on the jury trying Frank Cowperwood for embezzlement in 1871.

Glenn, Dr. *An American Tragedy.* A physician of the Gloversville, New York, area whom Roberta Alden consults in search of an abortion.

Goelet, Robert. "When the Old Century Was New." An iron-
monger in New York in the year 1801.

Goldfarb, Mitchell. *The "Genius."* The Sunday editor of a Chicago
newspaper on which Eugene Witla is employed.

Golden, Clifford (Clyde Griffiths). *An American Tragedy.* See Griffiths, Clyde.

Golden, Mrs. Clifford (Roberta Alden). *An American Tragedy.* See
Alden, Roberta.

Goole. *Fine Furniture.* The assistant to Olaf Saxton, manager of
the logging camp at Red Ledge.

Goujon, George. "Old Rogaum and His Theresa." A boy friend of
Myrtle Kenrihan.

Gove, Mabel. "The Second Choice." A girl friend of Shirley.

Graham, Carl (Clyde Griffiths). *An American Tragedy.* See Griffiths,
Clyde.

Graham, Mrs. Carl (Roberta Alden). See Alden, Roberta.

Gray, Fletcher. *The Financier.* A partner in the Philadelphia import-
ing firm of Cable & Gray who advises Frank Cowperwood
on his first art purchases; when Cowperwood's Philadelphia home is auctioned, Gray buys heavily from among the
treasures.

Greasadick, Henry. "The Victor." A competitor of J. H. Osterman
in the oil fields; he is financially ruined.

Greaves, Montague. *The Stoic.* An English contractor and railroad
builder who invests in the Traffic Electrical Company and
thus has an interest in the Charing Cross-Hampstead subway
planned by Frank Cowperwood.

Gregg, Gabriel. *An American Tragedy.* A justice of the peace before
whom Clyde Griffiths is brought for arraignment following
his arrest for the murder of Roberta Alden.

Gregory, Edward. "Will You Walk into My Parlor?" A New York
City politician who is resident at the Triton Hotel on Long
Island for the summer.

Gregory, Mrs. Edward (Emily). "Will You Walk into My Parlor?"
The wife of Edward Gregory; she visits her ill parents while
her husband resides on Long Island.

Grelizan. *The Stoic.* A clown from the Trocadero who entertains the
Frank Cowperwoods and Bruce Tollifer at a private party
at Orsignat's in Paris.

Gridley, G. A. "The Victor." An engineer employed by the financier, John H. Osterman.

Grier, Rhees. *The Titan.* A Chicago sculptor, member of the group cultivated by Aileen Cowperwood after her social repudiation by the city's wealthy and powerful families.

Griffiths, Asa. *An American Tragedy.* An itinerant missionary, the ineffectual father of Clyde Griffiths.

Griffiths, Bella. *An American Tragedy.* The younger daughter of Samuel Griffiths of Lycurgus, New York.

Griffiths, Clyde. *An American Tragedy.* The hero of the novel, drawn toward a life of ease and luxury, eventually executed for the murder of Roberta Alden. At various times, to cover his identity, he appears under these aliases: Baker, Clifford Golden, Carl Graham, and Harry Tenel.

Griffiths, Elvira. *An American Tragedy.* Clyde's mother, a deeply religious woman, steadfast in believing her son innocent of murdering Roberta Alden.

Griffiths, Frank. *An American Tragedy.* Clyde's younger brother, the youngest child of Asa and Elvira Griffith.

Griffiths, Gilbert. *An American Tragedy.* The son of Samuel Griffiths of Lycurgus, New York; he is Clyde's cousin; the two are somewhat of an age and closely resemble each other in appearance.

Griffiths, Hester "Esta." *An American Tragedy.* Clyde's sister, eldest child of Asa and Elvira Griffiths, who runs away from home with an itinerant actor and is abandoned by him when pregnant.

Griffiths, Julia. *An American Tragedy.* Clyde's sister, the younger daughter of Asa and Elvira Griffiths.

Griffiths, Myra. *An American Tragedy.* The eldest daughter of Samuel Griffiths of Lycurgus, New York; she is some three years older than her cousin Clyde.

Griffiths, Russell. *An American Tragedy.* The illegitimate son of Esta Griffiths; he is raised as their own by Asa and Elvira Griffiths.

Griffiths, Samuel. *An American Tragedy.* A brother of Asa Griffiths; he is a prosperous shirt and collar manufacturer of Lycurgus, New York.

Griffiths, Mrs. Samuel. *An American Tragedy.* An aunt of Clyde Griffiths.

Grund, Francis J. *The Financier.* The notorious post-Civil War lobbyist and speculator whose story is recounted by Frank Cowperwood's father while the financier is in his impressionable boyhood.

Gurney, Forbes. *The Titan.* A young playwright and poet in the artistic set of Chicago; as Stephanie Platow's lover, he is a romantic rival of Frank Cowperwood.

Haatstaedt. *The Titan.* A neighbor to the Frank Cowperwoods in Chicago.

Haatstaedt, Mrs. *The Titan.* A friend of Aileen Cowperwood; she remains friendly after Aileen's social repudiation but, not being socially prominent, is unable to provide her friend with the entry into the homes of the wealthy and powerful which she covets.

Haddonfield, Lord. *The Stoic.* A Britisher who entertains Frank Cowperwood at his home, Beriton Manor, near Hardown Heath in Shropshire.

Hadjaz, Al. "Khat"; "The Prince Who Was a Thief." A cook in the Moslem city of Hodeidah. See also Hajjaj, Al.

Hadley, Brentwood. *The "Genius."* A friend at whose home Suzanne Dale is visiting when Eugene Witla first declares his love for her.

Haeckelheimer, Joseph. *The Titan.* A New York financier, member of the firm of Haeckelheimer, Gotloeb & Company, with whom Judah Addison sounds out Frank Cowperwood's reputation in the East and with whom Cowperwood later arranges a pact for financial support.

Haguenin, Augustus M. *The Titan.* The Editor of the Chicago *Press;* he befriends Cowperwood until he discovers that the financier has seduced his daughter.

Haguenin, Cecily. *The Titan.* A Chicago editor's daughter who for a time becomes Frank Cowperwood's mistress.

Haifa. "Khat"; "The Prince Who Was a Thief." A tobacco tramp in the city of Hodeidah.

Hajjaj, Al. "Khat"; "The Prince Who Was a Thief." A cook in the city of Hodeidah. See also Hadjaz, Al.

Hall, Frank A. *Sister Carrie.* A resident of the Ogden Place apartment house in which Carrie Meeber lives with Charles Drouet in Chicago.

Hall, Mrs. Frank A. *Sister Carrie.* Chicago neighbor and friend of Carrie Meeber.

Haley. *An American Tragedy.* The superintendent of the Union League

Club of Chicago at the time that Clyde Griffiths is employed there as a bellboy.

Hammond. *Jennie Gerhardt.* A glass manufacturer, the employer of William Gerhardt.

Hand, Hosmer. *The Titan.* A Chicago financier, inimical to Frank Cowperwood.

Hand, Mrs. Hosmer (Caroline Barrett). *The Titan.* A financier's young wife, who becomes one of Frank Cowperwood's mistresses.

Hansen, Eric. *The Stoic.* The Norwegian skipper of the *Pelican*, on which Frank Cowperwood and Berenice Fleming cruise the fjords.

Hanson, Sven C. *Sister Carrie.* Carrie Meeber's brother-in-law, a cleaner of refrigerator cars at the Chicago stockyards.

Hanson, Mrs. Sven C. ("Minnie"). *Sister Carrie.* Carrie Meeber's older sister, with whom she lives when she first goes to Chicago.

Harmon, Jacob. *The Financier.* A Philadelphia alderman who works under the direction of the political boss, Edward Strobik.

Harriet. *An American Tragedy.* A socially prominent family who maintain a lodge at Twelfth Lake in the Adirondacks which Clyde Griffiths visits.

Harriet, Frank. *An American Tragedy.* A member of Sondra Finchley's social set in Lycurgus, New York, and at Twelfth Lake.

Harrigan, Rosalie. *The Stoic.* An actress in New York; she is the girl friend of Bruce Tollifer before his employment by Frank Cowperwood.

Harry. "Fulfilment." The multimillionaire manufacturer husband of Ulrica.

Hartley. *The Stoic.* An assistant to Jamieson, Frank Cowperwood's private secretary.

Hathaway, Constance. *The Stoic.* A London actress who is a guest at Beriton Manor while Cowperwood visits Lord Haddonfield there.

Hatton, Francis. "Married." A New York sculptor, friend of Duer Wilde.

Hauptwanger, Edward. "Typhoon." The son of a coal dealer.

Hauptwanger, Jacob. "Typhoon." A coal dealer in the Zobels' neighborhood; he is Edward's father.

Haverford, William. *The "Genius."* An Engineer of Maintenance of Way who employs Eugene Witla as a laborer on the railroad during his recuperation from neurasthenia.

Hawkesberry, Colonel. *The Stoic.* A resident of Wimbledon who
gives Frank Cowperwood suggestions as to cottages along
the Thames, one of which he might lease as a home for
Berenice Fleming; in time he becomes a good friend of
Berenice.

Hayes, Carter. *The "Genius."* An advertising man whom Eugene
Witla employs at the United Magazine Corporation.

Haymaker, Ethelberta. "Free." See Kelso, Mrs. John (Ethelberta
Haymaker).

Haymaker, Rufus. "Free." A New York architect who dreams of
being free from his marriage.

Haymaker, Mrs. Rufus (Ernestine). "Free." An architect's wife;
after a long illness she dies, too late satisfying her husband's
wish to be free of her.

Haymaker, Wesley. "Free." The son of Rufus and Ernestine Haymaker.

Haymaker, Mrs. Wesley (Irma De Gaud). "Free." The daughter of
George and Mrs. De Gaud.

Hedden, Major Wickham. *The Titan.* The father of Hattie Starr,
grandfather of Berenice Fleming.

Hedden, Nannie. *The Titan; The Stoic.* See Carter, Mrs. Ira George.

Hegglund, Oscar. *An American Tragedy.* One of Clyde Griffiths'
fellow bellboys at the Green-Davidson Hotel in Kansas City.

Heit, Fred. *An American Tragedy.* The coroner of Cataraqui County,
New York; he examines the body of Roberta Alden after
her drowning.

Heit, Mrs. Fred (Ella). *An American Tragedy.* The wife of the Cataraqui County Coroner.

Henderson. "St. Columba and the River." The engineer on the crew
building a tunnel beneath the Hudson River.

Henshaw, Philip. *The Stoic.* A British contractor and railway builder
who invests in the Traffic Electrical Company's project to
build a subway from Charing Cross to Hampstead.

Hibberdell, Mrs. *The "Genius."* Eugene Witla's landlady in Riverwood, New York.

Hibbs, Harry. *The Financier.* A Philadelphian who is physically
assaulted by Callum Butler for spreading the report that his
sister Aileen and Frank Cowperwood are lovers.

Higby, Paul. *An American Tragedy.* One of Clyde Griffiths' fellow
bellboys at the Green-Davidson Hotel in Kansas City.

Higgins, Wash. *An American Tragedy.* An inmate of Death Row in

Auburn Prison during Clyde Griffiths' incarceration.

Hillegan, Charles. *The Financier.* A Philadelphia contractor selected to serve on the jury trying Frank Cowperwood for embezzlement in 1871.

Hinsdale, Jessie Belle. *The Titan.* A mistress of Frank Cowperwood.

Hoagland, Mrs. *Sister Carrie.* A member of the cast of "Under the Gaslight" in which Carrie Meeber plays her first stage role.

Hobsen, Woodruff. *The "Genius."* A prominent railroad engineer in New York who is instrumental in finding employment for Eugene Witla while he recuperates from neurasthenia.

Hoecksema, Stanislau. *The Titan.* A prominent Chicago furrier.

Hoecksema, Mrs. Stanislau. *The Titan.* A social friend of Aileen Cowperwood who remains loyal to her after her repudiation by the leaders of Chicago society.

Hohstauffer, Elizabeth. "Typhoon." An aged German spinster who keeps a private religious school attended by Ida Zobel.

Hokutt, Walter. *The Bulwark.* A boyhood acquaintance of Solon Barnes; he and Solon are opponents in a wrestling match.

Hooper, Dr. *The Titan.* The President of the University of Chicago with whom Frank Cowperwood deals in donating his telescope to that institution soon after 1890.

Hopkins, Marshall. *Jennie Gerhardt.* A resident of the Columbus House hotel in Columbus, Ohio, in 1880.

Howard, Mrs. Ruth. *An American Tragedy.* See Alden, Roberta.

Howe, Horace. *The "Genius."* The "dean" of the art staff on the Chicago Newspaper where Eugene Witla works; he undertakes to teach Eugene personally.

Hubbard. *An American Tragedy.* The proprietor of Gun Lodge at Big Bittern lake where Clyde Griffiths and Roberta Alden stay on the night before Roberta's death.

Hubby, Ella F. *The Titan.* The daughter of a Chicago commission merchant; she is one of Frank Cowperwood's mistresses.

Huddleston, Henry. *The Titan.* A Chicago soap manufacturer.

Huddleston, Mrs. Henry. *The Titan.* A neighbor to the Frank Cowperwoods in Chicago.

Huldah. "The Hand." The black servant who confirms Davidson's suspicion that the mark on his ceiling is the imprint of a hand.

Hull, Phineas. *The Titan.* A member of Hull and Stackpole, bankers and brokers of Chicago; in 1896 he is a partner in the attempt to create a match trust, which ends in the bankruptcy of American Match and a financial triumph for Frank Cowperwood.

Hursted, Albert. *The Financier.* A Philadelphia burglar who in 1872 is sentenced for breaking and entering during the same court session at which Frank Cowperwood is sentenced for embezzlement.

Hurstwood, George W. *Sister Carrie.* The Manager of Fitzgerald and Moy's saloon in Chicago; he steals from his employers, runs off to New York with Carrie Meeber, loses his money and employment, and ends life a suicide. In Montreal he uses the alias of Murdock and in New York the alias of Wheeler.

Hurstwood, Mrs. George W. (Julia). *Sister Carrie.* The wife of George Hurstwood; when she discovers his relationship with Carrie Meeber, she divorces him.

Hurstwood, George W., Jr. *Sister Carrie.* The son of George and Julia Hurstwood.

Hurstwood, Jessica. *Sister Carrie.* The daughter of George and Julia Hurstwood.

Hussein. "Khat." A wood peddler in the city of Hodeidah.

Hussein, Prince. "The Prince Who Was a Thief." The hero of the story; when kidnapped by thieves, he is renamed Abou.

Hyssop, Hon. Walter Melville. *The Titan.* The Editor of both the Chicago *Transcript* and the Chicago *Mail;* he is inimical to Frank Cowperwood and friendly to his rival, Norman Schryhart.

Ike. "The Cruise of the 'Idlewild.'" A blacksmith's helper who is made Bos'n's mate on board the mythical ship "Idlewild."

Ingalls, Jeff. "Nigger Jeff." A black man accused of assaulting a white woman and subsequently lynched by a posse of vigilantes.

Israels, Webster. *The Titan.* A prominent Chicago meat packer.

Israels, Mrs. Webster. *The Titan.* A social friend of Aileen Cowperwood.

Isreals, Rev. Peter. *An American Tragedy.* The minister of the Diggby Avenue Congregational Church in Lycurgus, New York.

James, Dr. Jefferson. *The Stoic.* A New York physician; he treats Frank Cowperwood in his final illness.

Jamieson, Albert. *The Stoic.* The personal secretary of Frank Cowperwood.

Jansen, Jans. *The "Genius."* A newspaper art editor in New York who introduces Eugene Wilta to Norma Whitmore.

Jarkins, Willard. *The Stoic.* An American member of the firm of Jarkins, Kloorfain & Randolph, Frank Cowperwood's New York and London brokers.

Jaspers, Adlai. *The Financier.* The sheriff in charge of Frank Cowperwood at Moyamensing Prison in the days following his trial and preceding his sentencing.

Jeems, Sir Wilmington. *The Stoic.* A director of the District subway line in London.

Jefferson, Thomas. "When the Old Century Was New." The American patriot and future President.

Jeffords, Bill "One Eye." *The "Genius."* One of Eugene Witla's coworkers on the railroad crew at Riverwood, New York.

Jennings, Lester, Jr. *The Bulwark.* A classmate of Stewart Barnes at the Franklin Hall school.

Jephson, Reuben. *An American Tragedy.* A partner in the law firm of Belknap and Jephson, counsel to Samuel Griffiths; he retains the firm to defend Clyde Griffiths.

Jewell, Hilda. *The Titan.* A mistress of Frank Cowperwood in Chicago.

Joe. "The Cruise of the 'Idlewild.'" A millwright's assistant who is made the day watch on the mythical ship "Idlewild."

John "Old John." "The Cruise of the 'Idlewild.'" An engineer at the mill shop who is made Captain of the mythical ship "Idlewild."

Johns, Mrs. Althea. *The "Genius."* A friend of Myrtle Witla Bangs; she is a Christian Science practitioner whom Eugene Witla consults following Angela's death.

Johnson, Elverson. *The Stoic.* A member of the London firm of Rider, Bullock, Johnson & Chance, solicitor for the Traffic Electrical Company, and a counsel for Lord Stane.

Johnson, William. *The Titan.* A construction engineer with the North Chicago City Railway Company which Frank Cowperwood purchases.

Joseph. *The "Genius."* One of Eugene Witla's co-workers on the railroad crew at Riverwood, New York.

Joseph. *The Bulwark.* An aged retainer on the Thornbrough estate
near Philadelphia; he is a lifelong servant to Solon and
Benecia Barnes.
Jules, Jordan. *The Titan.* The President of the North Side Gas Company of Chicago; he opposes Frank Cowperwood's efforts
to control the company.

Kaempfaert, Solon. *The Titan.* A director of the North Chicago City
Railway Company which Frank Cowperwood purchases in
order in begin his career in streetcars.
Kaffrath, Edwin L. *The Titan.* A director of the North Chicago City
Railway Company; he is used by Frank Cowperwood in
order to gain control of that streetcar line.
Kain, Robert. *An American Tragedy.* A friend of Hortense Briggs in
Kansas City and thus a romantic rival of Clyde Griffiths.
Kalvin, Obadiah. *The "Genius."* The head of the Kalvin Publishing
Company of Philadelphia; he employs Eugene Witla as
managing editor of his prestigious concern.
Kane, Amy. *Jennie Gerhardt.* A sister of Lester Kane.
Kane, Archibald. *Jennie Gerhardt.* A Cincinnati carriage manufacturer;
he is Lester Kane's father.
Kane, Mrs. Archibald. *Jennie Gerhardt.* The mother of Lester Kane.
Kane, Imogene. *Jennie Gerhardt.* See Midgely, Mrs. Jefferson (Imogene
Kane).
Kane, Lester. *Jennie Gerhardt.* The son of a prosperous Cincinnati
carriage builder who falls in love with Jennie Gerhardt and
for many years lives with her but does not marry her; to his
eventual remorse, he leaves Jennie in order to conform to the
provisions of his father's will and thereby preserve his
fortune.
Kane, Mrs. Lester (Letty Pace Gerald). *Jennie Gerhardt.* A youthful
sweetheart of Lester Kane who marries Malcolm Gerald and
later, following Mr. Gerald's death, meets Lester once again;
when Lester leaves Jennie Gerhardt he marries Mrs. Gerald,
but he is never able to feel for her the love he felt for Jennie.
Kane, Louise. *Jennie Gerhardt.* The sister of Lester Kane; she discovers
that he is living openly with Jennie Gerhardt in Chicago and
informs the rest of the family, notably the father, Archibald
Kane.
Kane, Robert. *Jennie Gerhardt.* The older brother of Lester Kane;

unlike Lester, he is an ambitious and calculating businessman.

Kane, Willard. *The Bulwark*. An artist living in Greenwich Village; he is Etta Barnes' lover.

Kar-Shem, Sultan. "The Prince Who Was a Thief." The ruler of Yemen and the father of Prince Hussein.

Kasson, Frewen. *The Financier*. The Chairman of the board of directors of the Third National Bank in Philadelphia; when Frank Cowperwood is convicted of embezzlement, Frewen accepts the resignation from the bank of his father, Henry Worthington Cowperwood.

Keane, Iris. *The Bulwark*. A classmate of Stewart Barnes at the Red Kiln School.

Keane, Kittie. *An American Tragedy*. A member of the crowd with whom Hortense Briggs associates in Kansas City.

Keene, Ambassador. *The Bulwark*. A friend of the Segar Wallinses.

Keene, Mrs. *The Bulwark*. The wife of the Ambassador.

Kelles, Adlar. *The Bulwark*. A youthful friend of Benecia Wallin.

Keene, Gatchard. "Chains." A one-time lover of Idelle Garrison.

Kellogg, Ira. *An American Tragedy*. The President of the Cataraqui County National Bank.

Kelly, Kathleen. *The Financier*. A maid in service to the Edward Butlers at their home in Philadelphia.

Kelso, Horner. "Free." The father-in-law of Ethelberta Haymaker Kelso.

Kelso, Mrs. Horner (Grace). "Free." The mother-in-law of Ethelberta Haymaker Kelso.

Kelso, John. "Free." The husband of Ethelberta Haymaker.

Kelso, Mrs. John (Ethelberta Haymaker). "Free." The daughter of Rufus and Ernestine Haymaker; she is married to John Kelso.

Kemerer. *An American Tragedy*. An employee of Samuel Griffiths; he is in charge of the shrinking room at the shirt and collar factory in Lycurgus.

Kendall, Roger. *The Financier*. The receiving overseer of Eastern Penitentiary in Philadelphia during Frank Cowperwood's incarceration there in 1872-73.

Kennedy, Francis. *The Titan*. A young newspaperman in the employ of Frank Cowperwood, who uses him as a means of spying upon his mistress Stephanie Platow and thus of discovering her defection to Forbes Gurney.

Kenny. *Sister Carrie*. A stockbroker friend of George Hurstwood whom Hurstwood encounters in Montreal while fleeing

Chicago with Carrie.

Kenny, Ruby. *The "Genius."* A nude model at the Chicago Art Institute; she becomes Eugene Witla's mistress.

Kenrihan, Mrs. "Old Rogaum and His Theresa." A neighbor to the Rogaums in New York.

Kenrihan, Myrtle. "Old Rogaum and His Theresa." A close companion of Theresa Rogaum in New York.

Kernocian, Jerry K. *An American Tragedy.* The general manager of the Renfrew House hotel in Utica, New York, who testifies at Clyde Griffiths' trial that he registered there as Clifford Golden.

Kerrigan, Patrick "Emerald Pat." *The Titan.* The small and dapper alderman from Chicago's second ward; he is suborned by Frank Cowperwood and works to promote his interests.

Kimber, Anthony. *The Bulwark.* An uncle of Solon Barnes.

Kimber, Laura. *The Bulwark.* The daughter of Anthony and Pheobe Kimber, cousin to Solon Barnes.

Kimber, Phoebe. *The Bulwark.* The sister of Hannah Barnes and wife of Anthony Kimber.

Kimber, Rhoda. *The Bulwark.* See Wallin, Mrs. Segar, Jr.

Kingsbury, Ranse. *The Bulwark.* A Trenton, New Jersey, friend of Orville Barnes.

Kingsland, Duane. *The Titan.* A wholesale flour merchant in Chicago.

Kingsland, Mrs. Duane. *The Titan.* A social friend of Aileen Cowperwood in Chicago.

Kingsland, Henry. *The "Genius."* See Witla, Eugene.

Kinsella. "Sanctuary." Madeleine's father, a contentious and seldom-employed man.

Kinsella, Arthur. *An American Tragedy.* One of Clyde Griffiths' fellow bellboys at the Green-Davidson hotel in Kansas City.

Kinsella, Frank. "Sanctuary." A brother of Madeleine.

Kinsella, Madeleine. "Sanctuary." An innocent girl brought near to destruction by the slum environment in which she lives; eventually Madeleine seeks sanctuary from the world in a convent. At the time of her arrest for prostitution, she is using the alias Nellie Fitzpatrick.

Kinsella, Mrs. "Sanctuary." Madeleine's mother, a chronic drunkard.

Kinsella, Tina. "Sanctuary." A sister of Madeleine.

Kitchen, Judge. *The Financier.* A friend of Frank Cowperwood; during the panic of 1871 he agrees to lend the young financier $30,000.

Kitteredge. *The Stoic.* A subordinate of Frank Cowperwood in Chicago; he succeeds Henry de Sota Sippens as President of Cowperwood's Union Traction Company.

Klinkle. *An American Tragedy.* The proprietor of a drugstore in Kansas City where Clyde Griffiths works as a boy.

Klippert. "The Victor." An agent who acts for J. H. Osterman in establishing a foundation for the care of orphans.

Kloorfain, Willem. *The Stoic.* A Dutchman, the manager of the London office of the firm of Jarkins and Randolph, with whom Frank Cowperwood deals in his efforts to gain control of subway properties.

Knowles, Gardner. *The Titan.* The dramatic critic for the Chicago *Press*; he is a member of the Garrick Players and becomes the first lover of Stephanie Platow.

Koehler, Miss. "The Hand." A private nurse who serves Davidson while he is in a hospital for mental cases.

Kogel, Tina. *An American Tragedy.* A Kansas City girl who accompanies Paul Higby and Clyde Griffiths on the auto ride which ends with the death of a pedestrian.

Kolinsky, David. "A Story of Stories." A journalist on the New York *News* who writes under the pseudonym of David "Red" Collins.

Kortright, Eulalie. "When the Old Century Was New." The daughter of Madame Kortright.

Kortright, Madame. "When the Old Century Was New." A wealthy New York woman of the year 1801.

Kraut, Nicholas. *An American Tragedy.* The first deputy Sheriff of Cataraqui County, New York; he arrests Clyde Griffiths for the murder of Roberta Alden.

Kirby, Thomas. *The Financier.* A trusty in Eastern Penitentiary who assists with the reception of Frank Cowperwood as an inmate.

Kugel. *The Financier.* The President of the Third National Bank in Philadelphia; Henry Worthington Cowperwood works there.

Lambert, Dr. *The "Genius."* An obstetrical surgeon; he treats Angela Blue Witla in an attempt to save her life during childbirth.

Lambert, John. *An American Tragedy.* A druggist of Schenectady, New York, who testifies at Clyde Griffiths' trial that Clyde attempted to purchase medicine capable of producing a miscarriage.

Lanman, Chrystobel. *The Titan*. A friend of the Rhees Griers who accompanies them and Aileen Cowperwood to the Alcott gambling casino in Chicago.

Lansing, Miss. *The Bulwark*. A botany teacher at the Chadd's Ford school, which is attended by Etta Barnes.

La Porte. *The Bulwark*. A minimal Quaker, father of Volida La Porte.

La Porte, Volida. *The Bulwark*. A Wisconsin girl who attends the school at Chadd's Ford and becomes a friend of Etta Barnes, later influencing her to run away from home.

La Rue, Henry. *The "Genius."* An art dealer in New York who takes Eugene Witla's paintings to sell on consignment.

Laughlin, Peter. *The Titan*. A wheat and corn dealer and member of the Board of Trade in Chicago; he becomes Frank Cowperwood's first business partner in Chicago.

Laverty, Michael. *"St. Columba and the River."* The second foreman on the crew tunneling beneath the Hudson River.

Ledwell, Mrs. Josephine. *The Titan*. A mistress of Frank Cowperwood in Chicago.

Leigh, Walter. *The Financier*. A member of Drexel & Co. in Philadelphia to whom Frank Cowperwood goes for counsel and aid in the panic of 1871.

Leeks. *The Stoic*. The acting chairman of the District Railway in London at the time of Frank Cowperwood's fatal illness.

Lewis, Toma. *The Titan*. One of Frank Cowperwood's mistresses in Chicago.

Liggett. *An American Tragedy*. The chief of accounting at Samuel Griffiths' shirt and collar plant in Lycurgus, New York.

Liggett, Miss. *"The Hand."* A hospital nurse whom Davidson tells about his persecution by the dead Mersereau.

Litlebrown, Henry C. *The "Genius."* A divisional engineer on the railroad at Yonkers, New York, who puts Eugene Witla to work as a part of his cure for neurasthenia.

Little, Barnabas. *The Bulwark*. A youthful friend of Benecia Wallin Barnes.

Lincoln, Dr. *An American Tragedy*. A physician of Coldwater, New York, who is invited to participate in the autopsy on Roberta Alden.

Lord, Taylor. *The Titan*. A Chicago architect, a social friend of Frank Cowperwood and the designer of his Chicago mansion.

Lucas, Mayor Walden H. *The Titan*. The Mayor of Chicago, 1897-98; he is an opportunist but resists Frank Cowperwood's efforts to suborn him.

Lukash, Philip. *The Financier.* A Philadelphia coal merchant who serves on the jury trying Frank Cowperwood for embezzlement in 1871.

Lund, Foster. *An American Tragedy.* The foreman of the jury trying Clyde Griffiths for the murder of Roberta Alden.

Lutz. *An American Tragedy.* The last name of two brothers who are proprietors of the undertaking establishment in Bridgeburg which brings Roberta Alden's body back from Gun Lodge.

Lyle, Jonas. *The "Genius."* A journalist who works at the head desk of the composing room of the *Morning Appeal* in Alexandria, Illinois, during Eugene Witla's boyhood.

Lynde, Polk. *The Titan.* A playboy philanderer, son of a Chicago reaper manufacturer, who for a brief time in the early 1890s becomes the lover of Aileen Cowperwood.

Lynnwood, Rexford. *The Stoic.* An American sculptor who designs a marble tomb for Frank Cowperwood in Brooklyn's Greenwood Cemetery.

MacDonald, General. *The Titan.* The Editor of the Chicago *Inquirer*, inimical to Frank Cowperwood.

MacDonald, Truman Leslie. *The Titan.* The son of General MacDonald and his successor on *The Inquirer*; he offers to support Frank Cowperwood's efforts to obtain the La Salle Street tunnel in return for $50,000 in North Chicago Subway stock.

McEwen, Robert. *"McEwen of the Shining Slave Makers."* The hero of the story; he has a dream in which he joins the world of ants playing about his feet.

McGarren, Harry. *Sister Carrie.* The managing editor of the Chicago *Times*; he is a friend of George Hurstwood.

McGlathery, Dennis. *"St. Columba and the River."* An Irish immigrant who earns his living as a sand hog on the work crew tunneling beneath the Hudson River.

McGlathery, "Spat." *The Financier.* A neighborhood bully in Philadelphia who attempts, unsuccessfully, to intimidate Frank Cowperwood.

McHugh. *The "Genius."* A New York artist who shares a studio in Waverly Place with Eugene Witla.

McKenty, John J. *The Titan.* A political boss in Chicago who influences the mayor to award Frank Cowperwood a franchise for his gas company.

McKibben, Kent Barrows. *The Titan*. A Chicago lawyer who helps
Frank Cowperwood to set up dummy gas companies in Hyde
Park and South Side Chicago.

McMillan, Rev. Duncan. *An American Tragedy*. A Syracuse, New York,
minister; Elvira Griffiths persuades him to visit Clyde in
Auburn Prison.

Madenda, Carrie. *Sister Carrie*. See Meeber, Caroline.

Maguire, Officer. "Old Rogaum and His Theresa." A policeman
in the Rogaums' district of New York.

Major, Dr. "The Hand." The chief physician at the hospital in
which Davidson is treated.

Makin, Dr. *Jennie Gerhardt*. A Chicago physician who treats old
Gerhardt in his last illness.

Manigault. *An American Tragedy*. A law student who assists Orville
Mason to prepare the case against Clyde Griffiths.

Manning. *Jennie Gerhardt*. A storekeeper in Columbus, Ohio, from
whom Senator Brander orders Christmas supplies for the
Gerhardt family.

Manuel. *The Financier*. The body servant of Frank Cowperwood's
Uncle Seneca Davis.

Marchbanks, Oliver. *The Titan*. An employee of Frank Cowperwood;
he is assigned the task of suborning Mayor Chaffee Thayer
Sluss by trapping him in a sex affair with Claudia Carlstadt.

Marchwood. *The "Genius."* The Editor of the *International Review*, one
of the magazines published by the United Magazine Corporation which Eugene Witla heads.

Marie. "The Old Neighborhood." The wife of the ambitious, unnamed hero of the story, who is abandoned by him after the
deaths of their two young sons.

Marlborough, Duchess of. *The Stoic*. A guest, along with Frank
Cowperwood and Berenice Fleming, on Lord Stane's yacht
Iola.

Maris, Lorna. *The Stoic*. A distant relative of Frank Cowperwood
who introduces herself to him in Baltimore and subsequently
becomes his mistress.

Marr, Grace. *An American Tragedy*. A girl friend of Roberta Alden;
she persuades Roberta to find employment in Lycurgus.

Marsh, Richard. *The Financier*. A Philadelphia florist selected for
the jury which tries Frank Cowperwood for embezzlement
in 1871.

Martin, Rufus. *An American Tragedy*. The second cook at Bear Lake,

New York; he testifies at Clyde Griffiths' trial that he saw
Clyde kissing Sondra Finchley, known during the trial only
as "Miss X."

Martinson, Gilbert. *The Financier.* An agent of the Pinkerton Detective Agency of New York; he is employed by Edward Butler to ferret out the truth about his daughter's alleged affair with Frank Cowperwood.

Maru. "McEwen of the Shining Slave Makers." A Sanguinea ant warrior.

Marvin, Judge. *The Financier.* A judge of the Pennsylvania Supreme Court; he hears Frank Cowperwood's appeal for a new trial and favors granting it.

Mason, Martin. *The Bulwark.* The President of the bank in Dukla; he hires young Solon Barnes as a clerk/teller.

Mason, Orville W. *An American Tragedy.* The District Attorney of Cataraqui County, New York; he is in charge of the prosecution in Clyde Griffiths' trial for murder.

Mathews, Jeremiah. *The "Genius."* A member of the newspaper art staff in Chicago, a co-worker of Eugene Witla.

Mathews, Sheriff. "Nigger Jeff." He leads the posse which captures and jails Jeff Ingalls; later, he is unsuccessful in opposing the vigilantes who take Jeff from jail and lynch him.

Matjes, Otto. *The Titan.* A director of the North Chicago City Railway Company, which Frank Cowperwood operates.

Maurer, Ada. *The Bulwark.* A girl friend of Stewart Barnes.

Meeber, Caroline "Carrie." *Sister Carrie.* Heroine of the novel, who rises from sweatshop labor to success on the musical comedy stage. She is known also as Carrie Madenda, a name which is given her by Charles Drouet when she appears in the amateur theatrical "Under the Gaslight" in Chicago and which she later adopts as a stage name. When George Hurstwood takes her to Montreal, he registers her as Mrs. G. W. Murdock; and while she is living in New York with Hurstwood, she is known as Mrs. Wheeler, since he has adopted the name Wheeler in order to avoid having his past revealed publicly.

Merrill, Anson. *The Titan.* A dry-goods prince, the leading merchant of Chicago and an enemy of Frank Cowperwood.

Merrill, Mrs. Anson (Nellie). *The Titan.* A woman who discovers the truth regarding Frank and Aileen Cowperwood's past lives in Philadelphia; she works actively, and successfully, to ruin them socially in Chicago.

Mersereau. "The Hand." The partner of Davidson in the Klondike
    and other prospecting sites; he is killed by Davidson and
    supposedly revenges himself by haunting Davidson there-
    after.
Mews, Joseph. The "Genius." A co-worker with Eugene Witla on the
    railroad crew at Riverwood, New York.
Middleton, Dr. The Stoic. Lord Stane's personal physician at Trege-
    sal, his country home.
Midgely, Jefferson. Jennie Gerhardt. The husband of Imogene Kane.
Midgely, Mrs. Jefferson (Imogene Kane). Jennie Gerhardt. A sister
    of Lester Kane.
Miller, Edward. The Bulwark. The proprietor of a market in Dukla,
    near Philadelphia.
Miller, Greta. An American Tragedy. A friend of Hortense Briggs and
    Louise Ratterer; like them, she works in a Kansas City shop.
Miller, Townsend. The "Genius." An editor at the Kalvin Publishing
    Company in Philadelphia, where Eugene Witla is employed.
Miller, Mrs. Townsend. The "Genius." A friend of Angela Blue Witla
    in Philadelphia.
Millice. Sister Carrie. The man who at the Elks lodge in Chicago aids
    the director of the amateur theatrical "Under the Gaslight"
    in which Carrie Meeber appears.
Miriza. "The Prince Who Was a Thief." The wife of the master
    thief Yussuf.
Mitchell, Dr. An American Tragedy. A Bridgeburg, New York, phy-
    sician who is asked to examine the body of Roberta Alden
    after her drowning.
Mitchly, Henry. The "Genius." The manager of People's Furniture
    Company; he employs Eugene Witla as a driver.
Mollenhauer, Alta. The Financier. A daughter of Henry and Mrs.
    Mollenhauer.
Mollenhauer, Felicia. The Financier. A daughter of Henry and Mrs.
    Mollenhauer.
Mollenhauer, Henry A. The Financier. A financier; he is a political
    power in Philadelphia in the 1860s and 1870s.
Mollenhauer, Mrs. Henry A. The Financier. The wife of the financier;
    she invites Aileen Butler on a trip to Europe in 1871 as a
    means of getting her out of Philadelphia during Frank
    Cowperwood's trial.
Montague. The Financier. See Cowperwood, Frank Algernon.
Montague, Mrs. The Financier. See Cowperwood, Mrs. Frank
    Algernon (Aileen Butler).

Morgan, Mrs. *Sister Carrie.* A Chicagoan who plays the role of
Pearl in the Chicago Elks lodge amateur theatrical "Under
the Gaslight."

Morgenbau, Adolph. *The "Genius."* A publisher who suggests that
Eugene Witla apply as art director to the Summerfield Advertising Agency; Eugene secures this remunerative post,
and later Morgenbau hires him for an even better job at the
United Magazine Corporation.

Morison, Sagar. *Sister Carrie.* A friend of George Hurstwood who
accompanies him to the production of "Under the Gaslight"
in which Carrie Meeber appears.

Morris, Melville Ogden. "Married." The curator of a museum of
fine arts in New York; he is a friend of Duer Wilde.

Morris, Mrs. Melville Ogden. "Married." A friend of Marjorie Wilde,
in whose simple presence, unlike that of most of her husband's artistic circle, Marjorie feels at ease.

Moultrie, Philip. *The Financier.* A Philadelphia chicken and egg
wholesaler who is selected to serve on the jury trying Frank
Cowperwood for embezzlement in 1871.

Mowrer, Thomas. *An American Tragedy.* A convicted murderer; he
is an inmate of Auburn Prison while Clyde Griffiths is
incarcerated there.

Mulgannon, Terrence. *The Titan.* The general superintendent of
the North Chicago City Railway Company which Frank
Cowperwood purchases.

Murdock, G. W. *Sister Carrie.* See Hurstwood, George W.

Murdock, Mrs. G. W. *Sister Carrie.* See Meeber, Caroline "Carrie."

Murfree, Miss. *Jennie Gerhardt.* The nurse who tends Vesta Gerhardt
in her last illness.

Murtha, Patrick. "St. Columba and the River." A substitute ditcher
on the crew of sand hogs tunneling beneath the Hudson
River.

Nearjohn, Edward. *The Bulwark.* A classmate of Orville Barnes.

Newcomb, Earl. *An American Tragedy.* A typist and record clerk in
the coroner's office in Bridgeburg, New York.

Newcorn, Joseph. "Married." A self-made millionaire; he is an art
collector and a patron of the arts.

Newcorn, Mrs. Joseph. "Married." The wife of the millionaire, a simple woman, interested primarily in her children; she invites Marjorie Wilde to visit her.

Newton, George. *An American Tragedy.* A mill worker employed at Cranston Wickwire in Lycurgus, New York.

Newton, Mrs. George (Mary). *An American Tragedy.* The sister of Roberta Alden's good friend, Grace Marr; Roberta lives for a time at the Newtons' in Lycurgus.

Nickolas, Lucille. *An American Tragedy.* The girl accompanying Thomas Ratterer on the auto ride in Kansas City which ends with the accidental death of a pedestrian.

Nicholson, Miller. *An American Tragedy.* A Buffalo, New York, lawyer, convicted of murder and lodged in Death Row in the Auburn Prison.

Nicholson, Scott. *An American Tragedy.* A social friend of Sondra Finchley and member of her crowd in Lycurgus and the lake district.

Nikoforitch, Ruza. *An American Tragedy.* An employee in Clyde Griffiths' department of the shirt and collar factory in Lycurgus.

Norton, Fletcher. *The Financier.* A Philadelphia architect selected to serve on the jury trying Frank Cowperwood for embezzlement in 1871.

Nowack, Antoinette. *The Titan.* A secretary to Kent McKibben; she becomes Frank Cowperwood's private stenographer and then his mistress as well.

Nunnekamp, August. *The Financier.* A Philadelphian sentenced for horse stealing at the same court session during which Frank Cowperwood is sent to prison.

Oberwaltzer, Frederick. *An American Tragedy.* A Justice of the New York Supreme Court of the Eleventh Judicial District before whom Belknap and Jephson appear to request a change of venue for Clyde Griffiths.

O'Brien. *Jennie Gerhardt.* A Cincinnati lawyer in the service of Archibald Kane; he visits Jennie and explains to her the provisions of the will made by Lester's father.

Oeslogge. *Sister Carrie.* A New York neighborhood grocer whom George Hurstwood patronizes and, in his days of unemployment, attempts to cheat.

Og. "McEwen of the Shining Slave Makers." A Sanguinea ant warrior.

Oldshaw, Marcus. *The Financier*. An attorney retained by Edward Strobik to represent him as the president of the "common council" in prosecuting Frank Cowperwood for the city.

Olsen, Mrs. *Jennie Gerhardt*. A Chicago woman whom Jennie hires to care for Vesta at her home so that Lester Kane will not learn that she has a daughter.

Om. "McEwen of the Shining Slave Makers." A Sanguinea ant warrior.

Oman, Bab-al. "Khat." A restaurant keeper in the city of Hodeidah.

Ormsby, Dorothy. *The Titan*. One of Frank Cowperwood's mistresses.

Osborne, Lola. *Sister Carrie*. A New York chorus girl who befriends Carrie Meeber and from whom Carrie learns much in a practical way about employment on the stage.

Ostade. *The Stoic*. A member of the group assigned by Henry de Sota Sippens to investigate possibilities in London transit for Frank Cowperwood.

Osterman, John H. "The Victor." The financier hero of the story, a ruthless businessman who attempts to thwart his legal heirs by willing his immense fortune to a home for orphans.

Osterman, Mrs. John H. (Nadia Benda). "The Victor." The wife of the financier; against her husband's wishes, she manages to inherit his fortune.

Ottley, Irma. *The Titan*. A member of the Chicago amateur theatrical group, the Garrick Players.

Overman, Owen. *The "Genius."* A poet friend of Eugene Witla.

Pace, Letty. *Jennie Gerhardt*. See Kane, Mrs. Lester (Letty Pace Gerald).

Parch, George. *Fine Furniture*. A trimmer in the logging camp at Red Ledge; he is a friend of Clem Broderson.

Parker, Ira. *The Bulwark*. A youthful friend of Benecia Wallin.

Parrish, Jordan. *The Bulwark*. An investment broker, a cousin to the Wallinses.

Parrish, Kirkland. *The Bulwark*. A wealthy shipbuilder.

Parrish, Mrs. Kirkland. *The Bulwark*. The mother of Jordan Parrish; she is a socially prominent woman.

Parsons, Percy. *The Bulwark*. A classmate of Stewart Barnes at the Red Kiln school.

Patters, Viola. "Sanctuary." An inmate at the Sisterhood of the Good Shepherd along with Madeleine Kinsella; she is a prostitute who becomes Madeleine's confidante.

Patterson, Edna. *An American Tragedy.* A chambermaid at the Grass Lake Inn who testifies at Clyde Griffiths' trial that she saw him with a camera like that which purportedly struck Roberta Alden.

Patterson, Rae. *The Bulwark.* The girl friend of Stewart Barnes' classmate Lester Jennings.

Payderson, Judge Wilbur. *The Financier.* A Philadelphia judge; he presides at the 1871 trial of Frank Cowperwood for embezzlement from the city treasury.

Peoples, Myrtle. *The Bulwark.* A classmate of Dorothea Barnes.

Peter. "The Old Neighborhood." A son of the unnamed hero of the story; he dies as a boy from influenza.

Peters, John. *The "Genius."* An engineer on the railroad at Riverwood, New York; Eugene Witla works with him for a time.

Pethick, Richard. *The Financier.* An acquaintance of Callum Butler who spreads the story that Aileen Butler's relationship with Frank Cowperwood has been the true cause of Cowperwood's going to prison.

Petkansas, Hoda. *An American Tragedy.* An employee in Clyde Griffiths' department of the shirt and collar factory in Lycurgus.

Pettie, David. *The Financier.* The outgoing district attorney in Philadelphia in 1871; he informs Edward Butler that a charge of embezzlement may be lodged against Frank Cowperwood.

Pettingill, Blanche. *An American Tragedy.* A waitress at the Grass Lake House who testifies that she heard Clyde Griffiths arguing with Roberta Alden over the question of obtaining a marriage license.

Peyton, Mrs. *An American Tragedy.* A landlady in Lycurgus, New York; Clyde Griffiths takes lodgings at her house after he leaves Mrs. Cuppy's.

Pinski, Simon. *The Titan.* The alderman representing the Fourteenth Ward in Chicago, suborned by Frank Cowperwood but nevertheless forced by his constituency to vote against the Cowperwood franchise bill.

Pitcairn, Herbert. *The "Genius."* An agent for the Marquardt Trust Company, which is guardian of the estate Suzanne Dale has inherited from her father.

Pitti, Angelina. *An American Tragedy.* An employee in Clyde Griffiths' department of the shirt and collar factory in Lycurgus.

Platow, Isadore. *The Titan.* A wealthy Jewish furrier of Chicago; he meets Frank Cowperwood aboard a ship bound for Europe.

Platow, Mrs. Isadore (Susetta Osborn). *The Titan.* The Gentile mother of Stephanie Platow.

Platow, Stephanie. *The Titan.* The daughter of Isadore and Susetta Platow; she is an amateur actress in Chicago and becomes the mistress of Frank Cowperwood.

Pohlhemus, Andrew. *The Financier.* A Philadelphia broker with whom Frank Cowperwood is familiar during the time he works for Tighe and Company.

Pole, John. *An American Tragedy.* An Adirondack woodsman among the group who retrieve Roberta Alden's body from Big Bittern lake.

Polish Mary. *An American Tragedy.* An employee in Clyde Griffiths' department of the shirt and collar factory in Lycurgus.

Ponan. "McEwen of the Shining Slave Makers." A Sanguinea ant warrior.

Poole, Rita. *The Bulwark.* A student at Smith College; she is a classmate and friend of Rhoda Wallin.

Pope, Olive. *An American Tragedy.* An employee at the Cranston Wickwire plant in Lycurgus; she resides at the Newtons' while Roberta Alden lives there.

Prang. *The Bulwark.* A Federal bank examiner called in by Solon Barnes to investigate activities of the board of directors of the Traders and Builders Bank in Philadelphia.

Prendergast, Dorothy. *The Bulwark.* The hostess of a party in Wilmington, Delaware, attended by Stewart Barnes and a group of his classmates.

Prentice, Adelaide. *The Bulwark.* A friend of Isobel Barnes in Dukla, near Philadelphia.

Pringle. "The Hand." A Spiritualist; he talks with Davidson about clairvoyance and table rapping.

Pringle, Mrs. "The Hand." A Spiritualist; she is a friend of Davidson's sister and becomes acquainted with him through her.

Protus, Able. *The Financier.* A clerk in Judge Payderson's court in Philadelphia during the 1872 sentencing of Frank Cowperwood.

Purdy, Redmond. *The Titan.* A Chicago real-estate investor who disputes Frank Cowperwood's purchase of his land and buildings, only to find that Cowperwood has surreptitiously leveled the property on his own authority.

Pyne, Raymond. *The Titan.* The architect who plans a mansion for Frank Cowperwood along Millionaires Row on Fifth Avenue in New York.

Queeder, Bursay. "Phantom Gold." A farmer in Taney; he discovers that his supposedly worthless land is rich in zinc.

Queeder, Mrs. Bursay (Emma). "Phantom Gold." A farmer's wife who discovers the richness of her property despite her husband's efforts to keep that knowledge from her.

Queeder, Dode. "Phantom Gold." The eldest son of Bursay and Emma Queeder; he is infuriated when he discovers that his father has attempted to sell their zinc-rich farm and keep the profits for himself.

Queeder, Jane. "Phantom Gold." The daughter of Bursay and Emma Queeder.

Quincel, Harry. *Sister Carrie.* A prominent member of the Elks lodge in Chicago; he is in charge of the amateur production of "Under the Gaslight" in which Carrie Meeber appears.

Race, Matilda. "The Lost Phoebe." A neighbor of the Henry Reifsneiders.

Rafalsky, Judge. *The Financier.* A Justice of the Supreme Court of Pennsylvania who hears Frank Cowperwood's appeal for a new trial.

Raine, Ned. *The Bulwark.* A friend of the Segar Wallliises.

Rainer, Joe. *An American Tragedy.* An Adirondack woodsman who participates in the recovery of Roberta Alden's body from Big Bittern lake.

Rainey, Judge. *The Financier.* A Justice of the Supreme Court of Pennsylvania who hears Frank Cowperwood's appeal for a new trial and rejects it.

Rambaud, Alexander. *The Titan.* A pioneer railroader, President of the Chicago and Northwestern Railroad, who suggests to Frank Cowperwood that he investigate the business potential of Fargo, North Dakota, and the surrounding territory.

Rambaud, Mrs. Alexander. *The Titan.* A social friend of Aileen Cowperwood; she remains loyal despite the Cowperwoods' repudiation by social leaders of Chicago society.

Randolph. *The Stoic.* A member of the London firm of Jarkins, Kloorfain, and Randolph, agents for Frank Cowperwood in his effort to enter London transit.

Ratterer, Louise. *An American Tragedy.* The younger sister of Thomas Ratterer; she clerks in a Kansas City dry-goods store.

Ratterer, Mrs. *An American Tragedy.* The widowed mother of Louise and Thomas Ratterer.

Ratterer, Thomas. *An American Tragedy.* A bellboy at the Green-Davidson Hotel in Kansas City who becomes a close friend of Clyde Griffiths.

Reifsneider, Henry. "The Lost Phoebe." An aged farmer who loses his wife and, subsequently, his mind.

Reifsneider, Mrs. Henry (Phoebe Ann). "The Lost Phoebe." The wife of Henry Reifsneider; her death leaves him alone and causes his derangement.

Relihan, Terrence. *The Financier.* A Pennsylvania state senator who represents the interests of important Philadelphia financiers in the legislature.

Reystadt, Maria. *The Stoic.* The Czech-Hungarian widow of an Austrian military representative in France; she becomes a member of Bruce Tollifer's and Aileen Cowperwood's set in Paris.

Rider, Wellington. *The Stoic.* The Vice-Chairman of the Traffic Electrical Company in London, which Frank Cowperwood purchases in order to enter the subway field there; Rider also manages the estate of Lord Stane and handles legal business for the District Railway.

Riordan, Officer. *An American Tragedy.* A Rochester, New York, policeman who has murdered his wife and been sentenced to death; he is on Death Row in Auburn Prison at the time of Clyde Griffiths' incarceration there.

Ritter, Olive. *The Bulwark.* A friend of Steward Barnes; he meets her at a dance at Dorothy Prendergast's home.

Rivers, Arthur. *The Financier.* The floor man for Tighe & Co. on the Philadelphia Stock Exchange; Frank Cowperwood learns much from him about the operations of the exchange.

Rivers, Emily. *The Financier.* A sister of Arthur Rivers.

Roberts, Judge. *The Stoic.* A New York judge; he presides over the court case in which Aileen Cowperwood protests the official appraisal which has been made of her deceased husband's estate.

Robertson. *The Stoic.* A New York attorney who acts for Aileen
  Cowperwood during the time she is estranged from her
  husband.
Rodeheaver, Cosmo. *The Bulwark.* The son of a bookstore operator
  in Dukla, near Philadelphia; he is a friend of Stewart Barnes.
Rogaum. "Old Rogaum and His Theresa." A German butcher of
  New York, living in the area near Fourteenth Street.
Rogaum, Mrs. "Old Rogaum and His Theresa." The mother of
  Theresa; she attempts to mollify her husband's anger with
  their daughter.
Rogaum, Theresa. "Old Rogaum and His Theresa." The eighteen-
  year-old daughter of butcher Rogaum; she is locked out
  of their home by her father when she stays out beyond her
  curfew.
Rokes, Bud. *Fine Furniture.* A senior high-climber in the logging
  camp at Red Ledge; he is insulted when Opal Broderson
  objects to his wearing his boots into her home.
Rollins, Lem. "A Story of Stories." A train robber interviewed by
  Gus Binns and Red Collins.
Rose. *The Stoic.* A maid employed by Berenice Fleming while she
  is living at Pryor's Cove along the Thames.
Ross, Camuel F. *Jennie Gerhardt.* A Chicago real-estate man who inter-
  ests Lester Kane in a speculative land deal which envisions
  a new residential subdivision in the Halstead Street-Ashland
  Avenue area.
Roth, Frieda. *The "Genius."* An Alexandria, Illinois, girl with whom
  Eugene Witla is in love as a teenager.
Roth, George. *The "Genius."* A traveling salesman of Alexandria,
  Illinois.
Roth, Mrs. George (Anna). *The "Genius."* The mother of Frieda Roth.
Rubenstein, Isadore. *An American Tragedy.* The son of a clothing-
  store proprietor in Kansas City at whose establishment
  Hortense Briggs wishes Clyde Griffiths to purchase an
  expensive coat for her.
Russell, Charlotte. "Married." An artist friend of Duer Wilde in
  New York; Marjorie Wilde feels ill at ease in her presence
  and urges her husband to cultivate other, more conservative
  friends.
Rutter, Harvey. *The "Genius."* A rival of Eugene Witla for the affections of Stella Appleton.
Ryan. "The 'Mercy' of God." A contractor and politician, the father
  of Celeste and Marguerite.

Ryan, Celeste. "The 'Mercy' of God." The sister of Marguerite; by one of life's ironies, Celeste is born a beauty and thereby is a persistent reminder to Marguerite of her own plainness.

Ryan, Marguerite. "The 'Mercy' of God." A girl in whom the lack of physical beauty eventually proves to be deranging.

Sableworth, Adlar. *The Bulwark.* The first vice-president of the Traders and Builders Bank of Philadelphia, in which Solon Barnes has a substantial interest.

Sabinal, Victor Leon. *The Stoic.* A wealthy Argentinian expatriate living in Paris; he becomes a member of Bruce Tollifer and Aileen Cowperwood's set there.

St. Agnes, Sister. "Sanctuary." The superviser of the sewing room at the Sisterhood of the Good Shepherd, a home for wayward girls in which Madeleine Kinsella is lodged.

St. Bertha, Mother. "Sanctuary." The Mother Superior of the Sisterhood of the Good Shepherd in New York.

Saljerian. *The "Genius."* A Syrian living in Chicago; he is among the first of America's professional advertising agents.

Sampson. *The Financier.* Young Frank Cowperwood's immediate superior at Waterman & Co., his first employer in Philadelphia.

Saunders, Zillah. *An American Tragedy.* A stenographer in service to Orville Mason, District Attorney of Cataraqui County, New York.

Saxstrom, Olaf. *Fine Furniture.* The superintendent of the logging company established in Red Ledge.

Saxstrom, Mrs. Olaf. *Fine Furniture.* Wife of the superintendent of the logging company and thus the social leader of the camp; it is Mrs. Sexton whose position Opal Broderson challenges with her houseful of fine furniture.

Scain, Dr. "The Hand." A psychiatrist who treats Davidson for his persecution complex.

Scanlon. *The Financier.* See Butler, Edward Malia.

Scarr, Abington. *The Stoic.* The promoter of the Baker Street and Waterloo subway line in London.

Scattergood, Susan. *The Bulwark.* A youthful friend of Benecia Wallin and Solon Barnes.

Schaefer, Frank W. *An American Tragedy.* A clerk at the Renfrew House in Utica, New York, who testifies that Clyde Griffiths registered there with Roberta Alden as Mr. and Mrs. Clifford Golden.

Schlict, Lena "Dutch Lena." *An American Tragedy.* An employee in Clyde Griffiths' department of the shirt and collar factory in Lycurgus.

Schoof, Miss. *An American Tragedy.* An evangelist who works with Asa and Elvira Griffiths at their mission in San Francisco in the years following Clyde's execution.

Schreiber, Heinrich. *The Stoic.* The Captain of the *Kaiser Wilhelm der Grosse* during Frank Cowperwood's voyage to London in 1900.

Schryhart, Norman. *The Titan.* A Chicago financier; he is a formidable rival to Frank Cowperwood's interests and controls the anti-Cowperwood *Chronicle.*

Scott, Georgina. *The Bulwark.* A student at Vassar, a friend of Rhoda Wallin.

Seavey. "Nigger Jeff." The telegraph operator in Baldwin; reporter Elmer Davies uses his facilities when he turns in his story of the lynching.

Seay, S. Guy. *The Bulwark.* A director of the Traders and Builders Bank of Philadelphia, in which Solon Barnes has a substantial interest.

Secor. *An American Tragedy.* The manager of a drugstore in Kansas City to whom Clyde Griffiths applies for work.

Sells, Frederick "Freddie." *An American Tragedy.* An employee of General Electric in Schenectady, New York; he is a friend of Sondra Finchley.

Semple, Alfred. *The Financier.* The operator of a shoe store in Philadelphia

Semple, Mrs. Alfred (Lillian Wiggin). *The Financier; The Titan; The Stoic.* The wife of Alfred Semple, later his widow, and subsequently Mrs. Frank Algernon Cowperwood; they are divorced following Cowperwood's imprisonment for embezzlement.

Sempronia, Sister. *The Financier.* One of Aileen Butler's teachers at St. Agatha's convent school.

Sengstack, Abner. *The Financier.* The secretary to Henry Mollenhauer, the Philadelphia financier and political boss.

Severas, Luke. *The "Genius."* An art critic who favors Eugene Witla at the inception of his career and praises his first one-man show in the New York *Evening News.*

Severence, Lord. *The Stoic.* A friend of Lord Stane; he furnishes Berenice Fleming with advice on her proposed trip to India.

Severing, Judge. *The Stoic.* A New York judge; he presides over the litigation by means of which Aileen Cowperwood attempts to remove Jamieson as the executor of her deceased husband's estate.

Shanley, Michael. *The Stoic.* A one-time employee of Frank Cowperwood who accompanies him on a visit to the Père-Lachaise Cemetery in Paris.

Shannon, Dennis. *The Financier.* A lawyer, protégé of Edward Malia Butler; he is elected District Attorney in Philadelphia in 1871.

Shaughnessy. *Sister Carrie.* A New York saloonkeeper in whose establishment George Hurstwood purchases a partnership, only to lose his money when the premises are sold by the owner.

Sheridan, Albert. *Jennie Gerhardt.* The husband of Veronica Gerhardt.

Sheridan, Mrs. Albert (Veronica Gerhardt). *Jennie Gerhardt.* A sister of Jennie Gerhardt.

Shiel, Paul. *An American Tragedy.* One of Clyde Griffiths' fellow bellboys at the Green-Davidson Hotel in Kansas City.

Shirley. "The Second Choice." The heroine of the story, who is caught in the irony of loving a man who will not marry her and being proposed to by a man for whom she cares little.

Shoemaker, Marigold. *The Stoic.* See Brainerd, Mrs. Sidney (Marigold Shoemaker).

Shomel, Etelka. "Typhoon." A girl friend of Ida Zobel.

Shoop, Sim. *An American Tragedy.* A guide at Big Bittern lake in the Adirondacks; he is a witness to the presence in that area of Clyde Griffiths and Roberta Alden.

Short, Orrin. *An American Tragedy.* The proprietor of a gentlemen's haberdashery in Lycurgus of whom Clyde Griffiths asks advice in obtaining an abortion for Roberta Alden.

Shotmeyer, Philip. *The "Genius."* A neighbor to Eugene Witla in New York; he encourages Eugene to offer some of his paintings for sale to *Truth* magazine.

Showalter, Amos. *An American Tragedy.* A general-delivery clerk in Lycurgus; he testifies at Clyde Griffiths' trial that Clyde received letters in the mail from Roberta Alden.

Shuman, Zella. *An American Tragedy.* A girl friend of Clyde Griffiths' companion Walter Dillard.

Shurlock, Fred. *An American Tragedy.* An electrician in Lycurgus,

New York; he is a friend of Roberta Alden.

Sieberling, Albert. *An American Tragedy*. Clyde's superior at the drugstore soda fountain where he finds his first job at the age of fifteen in Kansas City.

Simpson, Davis. *The "Genius."* A nephew of Mrs. Hibberdell in Riverwood, New York.

Simpson, Senator Mark. *The Financier*. One of the three most powerful political leaders in Philadelphia in the 1870s.

Simms, Norrie. *The Titan*. The Secretary and Treasurer of the Douglas Trust and Savings Company in Chicago.

Simms, Mrs. Norrie (Bella). *The Titan*. A friend of Aileen Cowperwood in Chicago.

Sims, "Wash." *The Financier*. Frank Cowperwood's janitor at his Girard Avenue mansion in Philadelphia.

Sipe, Laura. *An American Tragedy*. Willard Sparser's girl friend on the automobile ride which ends with the accidental death of a pedestrian; as a result of this accident, Clyde Griffiths flees Kansas City.

Sippens, Henry de Sota. *The Stoic*. See Sippens, Henry De Soto.

Sippens, Henry De Soto. *The Titan; The Stoic*. A Lake View real-estate dealer who becomes Frank Cowperwood's chief agent in Chicago; in *The Stoic* (where his name unaccountably is spelled *de Sota* Sippens) he is sent to London to reconnoitre the subway situation preparatory to Cowperwood's entry into that field.

Sissel. *An American Tragedy*. The second deputy sheriff of Cataraqui County, New York.

Skeet, Watson. *The Titan*. A Chicago sculptor; he succeeds Polk Lynde as Aileen Cowperwood's lover.

Skelton, Mrs. *"Will You Walk into My Parlor?"* A theatrical-agency owner who is resident for the summer at the Triton Hotel on Long Island.

Skidmore, Ezra. *The Bulwark*. The President of the Traders and Builders Bank in Philadelphia.

Skinner, Onias C. *The Titan*. The President of the North Chicago City Railway Company, which Frank Cowperwood purchases.

Slack, Sheriff. *An American Tragedy*. The Sheriff of Cataraqui County, New York, site of Roberta Alden's death.

Sledd, Sutherland. *The Titan*. The general traffic-manager of the Southwestern Railway, headquartered in Chicago.

Sledd, Mrs. Sutherland. *The Titan.* A friend of Aileen Cowperwood.

Sluss, Chaffee Thayer. *The Titan.* The successful Republican candidate for Mayor of Chicago, c. 1892; he is anti-Cowperwood.

Smillie, Rudolph. *An American Tragedy.* A vice president at the Griffiths shirt and collar factory in Lycurgus, New York.

Smite, Joseph. *The "Genius."* A New York artist who shares a studio with Eugene Witla and McHugh in Waverly Place.

Smithson, Judge. *The Financier.* A Justice of the Pennsylvania Supreme Court who hears Frank Cowperwood's appeal for a new trial and opposes it.

Sohlberg, Harold. *The Titan.* A Danish violinist living in Chicago during the 1890s.

Sohlberg, Mrs. Harold (Rita Greenough). *The Titan.* A violinist's wife who becomes Frank Cowperwood's mistress; when Aileen Cowperwood discovers her husband's defection, she assaults Rita physically.

Sommerville, Mrs. *Jennie Gerhardt.* A neighbor of Jennie in the Hyde Park area of Chicago.

Southack, Senator John H. *The Titan.* A member of the Illinois state legislature; General Van Sickle and Joel Avery succeed in persuading him to introduce and support a bill which would grant Frank Cowperwood's streetcar lines a fifty-year franchise extension.

Sparkheaver, Bailiff. *The Financier.* The Bailiff in the Court of Quarter Sessions, Philadelphia, at the time of Frank Cowperwood's conviction for embezzlement.

Sparser, Willard. *An American Tragedy.* A friend of Clyde Griffiths in Kansas City; he borrows a Packard automobile and takes a group for a joy ride, the upshot of which is that a pedestrian is struck and killed, impelling Clyde to flee from the city.

Speyer. *The Stoic.* The great New York and London banking firm, agents for Frank Cowperwood in his London enterprise.

Sprull, Dr. *An American Tragedy.* An Albany, New York, physician invited to participate in the autopsy on Roberta Alden following her drowning.

Squires, Francis X. *An American Tragedy.* The captain of bellboys at the Green-Davidson Hotel in Kansas City.

Stackpole, Benoni. *The Titan.* A partner in Hull and Stackpole, bankers and brokers; he fails in his wish to create a match monopoly, and the failure of his American Match firm provides Frank Cowperwood with a great financial triumph in Chicago.

Stafford, Marjorie. *The Financier.* A girl friend of Frank Cowperwood during his youth in Philadelphia.

Stapley. *The Financier.* A bookkeeper working in the office of George W. Stener, Treasurer of Philadelphia.

Stane, Gordon Roderick, Lord. *The Stoic.* The son of the Earl of Stane; he is an important shareholder in the District Railway of London.

Stark, Arabella. *An American Tragedy.* A friend of Sondra Finchley.

Stark, Mark. *Fine Furniture.* A tree feller in the logging camp at Red Ledge who helps Clem Broderson move his new furniture into his house.

Stark, Mrs. Mark. *Fine Furniture.* A tree-feller's wife to whom Opal Broderson feels socially superior.

Starr, Hattie. *The Titan; The Stoic.* See Carter, Mrs. Ira George.

Stearns, Ollie. "Married." A New York contralto; she is one of Duer Wilde's friends with whom Marjorie Wilde feels ill at ease.

Steele, Vanda. *An American Tragedy.* A social friend of Sondra Finchley in Gloversville, New York.

Steele, Wallace. "Convention." A prominent newspaperman in a Mid-Western American city.

Steele, Mrs. Wallace (Estelle). "Convention." A faded and deranged woman who falls ill of poisoned candy which she has mailed to herself.

Steele, Rev. Willis. *The Stoic.* The rector of St. Swithin's Church in New York.

Steemberger. *The Financier.* The notorious beef speculator; Frank Cowperwood hears his story as a boy when his father speaks of it at home.

Steger, Harper. *The Financier; The Titan.* Frank Cowperwood's attorney in Philadelphia; he defends his client against the charge of embezzlement in 1871, and later he arranges for Cowperwood's divorce from Lillian Semple Cowperwood.

Steinmetz. *The Financier.* An engineer employed by the contracting firm owned by Edward Malia Butler.

Steinmetz, Mrs. *The Financier.* The wife of Butler's engineer; Aileen Butler is sent to stay with Mrs. Steinmetz and her husband at their home in West Chester in order that she will be away from Philadelphia during Frank Cowperwood's trial.

Stendahl, Mrs. Jacob. *Jennie Gerhardt.* A neighbor of Jennie and Lester Kane in the Hyde Park area of Chicago.

Stener, George W. *The Financier.* The City Treasurer of Philadelphia, first elected in 1864; he allows Frank Cowperwood to use city funds in a quasi-legal fashion and in 1871 is convicted, with Cowperwood, of embezzlement.

Stimson, Burton. *The Titan*. A Chicago lawyer who helps Frank
Cowperwood establish dummy gas companies in the West
Park and Douglas suburbs.

Stires, Albert. *The Financier*. The chief clerk employed in the office
of George W. Stener, City Treasurer of Philadelphia.

Stix, Jack. *The "Genius."* The foreman carpenter of the railroad crew
with which Eugene Witla works in Speonk, New York.

Stoddard, Althea. *The Bulwark*. See Barnes, Mrs. Orville (Althea
Stoddard).

Stoddard, Edward. *The Bulwark*. The son of Isaac Stoddard; he is a
classmate of Orville Barnes at the Oakwold school.

Stoddard, Mrs. Gilbert (Beryl Dana). "The Shadow." A woman who
attempts to pattern her life upon a novel she has chanced to
read.

Stoddard, Gilbert. "The Shadow." The mild clerk-hero of the story.

Stoddard, Gilbert, Jr., "Tickles." "The Shadow." The son of Gilbert
and Beryl Stoddard.

Stoddard, Isaac. *The Bulwark*. The father of Althea and Edward; he
is the owner of a prosperous pottery business in the Dukla
area near Philadelphia.

Stone, Avery. *The Financier*. An officer of Jay Cooke & Co. in Philadelphia; Frank Cowperwood consults him for aid and advice
during the panic of 1871.

Stone, Oliver. *The Bulwark*. A hardware dealer in Dukla, near
Philadelphia.

Stoneledge, Sir Charles. *The Stoic*. A London actor, guest of Lord
Haddonfield at his country estate, Beriton Manor, at the
time that Frank Cowperwood is visiting there.

Storm, Dr. "Free." The physician who treats the Haymaker family.

Stour, Walter. "Typhoon." A young man of the neighborhood, to
whom Ida Zobel is attracted.

Stover, Henry. *Jennie Gerhardt*. The adopted son of Jennie Gerhardt;
the name *Stover* is an alias.

Stover, J. G. *Jennie Gerhardt*. An invented name for Jennie Gerhardt's
nonexistent husband and for Vesta's father; *Stover* was Mrs.
William Gerhardt's maiden name.

Stover, Mrs. J. G. *Jennie Gerhardt*. See Gerhardt, Jennie.

Stover, Rose Perpetua. *Jennie Gerhardt*. Jennie's adopted daughter.

Stover, Vesta. *Jennie Gerhardt*. See Gerhardt, Wilhelmina Vesta.

Strake, Gordon. *The Financier.* An art dealer who sells Frank Cowperwood rare items for his collection; he buys back heavily when the Cowperwood home and its contents are auctioned.

Strobik, Edward. *The Financier.* A Philadelphia councilman, the tool of financier Henry Mollenhauer; he is called "The Dude" in political circles.

Styles, Wilson. *The Stoic.* A playwright who is a passenger aboard the *Kaiser Wilhelm der Grosse* during the voyage which takes the Frank Cowperwoods across the Atlantic in 1900.

Sudds, Jimmy. *The "Genius."* A blacksmith's helper on the railroad crew with whom Eugene Witla works at Riverwood, New York, during his recuperation from neurasthenia.

Sullivan, Lawrence. *"Typhoon"* A soda clerk in a drugstore; Ida Zobel has a crush on him during her teenage years.

Summerfield, Daniel Christopher. *"The "Genius."* The President of the Summerfield Advertising Agency; he is Eugene Witla's employer.

Summers, John. *The "Genius."* An employee on Benjamin Burgess' *Morning Appeal* in Alexandria, Illinois, during Eugene Witla's boyhood.

Swanson, Governor. *The Titan.* The immigrant governor of Illinois who refuses a bribe of $300,000 offered him through Judge Dickensheets in order to assure that he will not veto the franchise bill favoring Frank Cowperwood's streetcar lines.

Swartz, Bill. *An American Tragedy.* A woodsman who finds Clyde Griffiths' camera tripod under a log near Big Bittern lake; at Clyde's trial he testifies to that effect.

Swayne, Jack. *"Will You Walk Into My Parlor?"* The President of the Union Bank of Penyank who is in league with the mayor of an unnamed American city in crooked land deals.

Swenk, Ed. *An American Tragedy.* The third deputy sheriff of Cataraqui County, New York.

Swighort, "Dutch." *An American Tragedy.* An inmate of Auburn Prison at the time that Clyde Griffiths is incarcerated there.

Sword, Dr. A. K. *An American Tragedy.* A physician of Rehobeth, New York, who chances to be at Big Bittern lake when Roberta Alden's body is recovered and who later testifies in court that her wounds could have been received in the manner Clyde claims they were.

Tacksun, Sam. *An American Tragedy.* The Editor and Publisher of the Bridgeburg, New York, *Democrat.*

Taintor, Frank L. *Sister Carrie.* A friend of George Hurstwood in Chicago; they are together on the night that Hurstwood steals from Fitzgerald and Moy's.

Tanzer, Psyche. *The Bulwark.* A girl friend of Stewart Barnes' companion Victor Bruge; she dies during an auto ride with the boys when Bruge, unaware of her heart condition, gives her a potent tranquilizing drug.

Targool, Newton. *The Financier.* A broker on the Philadelphia Stock Exchange.

Tavistock, Arthur. *The Stoic.* An English bachelor; he becomes a close friend of Berenice Fleming and locates a home for her to lease along the Thames.

Taylor, Bart. *Sister Carrie.* A friend of Jessica Hurstwood; he inadvertently reveals to Mrs. Hurstwood that her husband has attended the performance of "Under the Gaslight" at the Elks lodge.

Taylor, Burchard. *An American Tragedy.* A member of the Lycurgus social set which gathers for the summer at Twelfth Lake in the Adirondacks.

Taylor, Violet. *An American Tragedy.* A member of the young social set which gathers for the summer at Twelfth Lake in the Adirondacks.

Temple, Myra. *The Bulwark.* A girl friend of Stewart Barnes' companion Victor Bruge.

Temple, Nina. *An American Tragedy.* A friend of Sondra Finchley and member of the summer social set at Twelfth Lake in the Adirondacks.

Templeton, Mrs. Anna. *The Stoic.* See Cowperwood, Lillian.

Tenel, Harry. *An American Tragedy.* See Griffiths, Clyde.

Tenet, Mrs. *The Bulwark.* A neighbor of the Solon Barnes family in Dukla, near Philadelphia.

Tenet, Regina. *The Bulwark.* A schoolmate of Dorothea Barnes.

Thomas, Washington B. *The Financier.* A wholesale flour merchant of Philadelphia who is selected to serve on the jury trying Frank Cowperwood for embezzlement in 1871.

Thompson. *The "Genius."* A lathe worker for the railroad; Eugene Witla works with him for a time in Riverwood, New York.

Thorne, Mrs. Judith. *The Stoic.* An acquaintance of Bruce Tollifer and Aileen Cowperwood in Paris and a member of their social set there.

Thorsen, Albert. *The Titan.* A director of the North Chicago City Railway Company, which Frank Cowperwood purchases.

Thurston, Floyd. *An American Tragedy.* A guest at the Cranstons' lodge on Twelfth Lake in the Adirondacks at the time of the Roberta Alden drowning.

Tiernan, Michael "Smiling Mike." *The Titan.* A Chicago saloon-keeper and political boss, Alderman from the First Ward; he attempts so far as possible to carry out Frank Cowperwood's wishes.

Tighe, Edward. *The Financier.* A Philadelphia broker; he is one of the first employers of Frank Cowperwood.

Tilney. "Will You Walk into My Parlor?" A real-estate plunger; he is the partner of an unnamed mayor engaged in shady land deals.

Tilton, Lord. *The Titan; The Stoic.* A Britisher who loans Frank Cowperwood the use of his yacht *Pelican* for touring Norway with Berenice Fleming.

Timberlake, Georgia. *The Titan.* A Chicago girl in whose home the city's Amateur Dramatic League has its beginning.

Tisdale, Joseph. *The Financier.* A retired glue manufacturer of Philadelphia who is selected to sit on the jury trying Frank Cowperwood for embezzlement in 1871.

Todd, Miss. *An American Tragedy.* An employee in Clyde Griffiths' department of the shirt and collar factory in Lycurgus.

Tollifer, Bruce. *The Stoic.* A Broadway hanger-on whom Frank Cowperwood engages as a hired companion for Aileen in order to camouflage his own continuing interest in Berenice Fleming.

Tollifer, Col. Wexford. *The Stoic.* The Carolina-born Army captain brother of Bruce Tollifer.

Tomlinson, Senator. *The Bulwark.* A friend of the Segar Wallinses.

Tomlinson, Mrs. *The Bulwark.* The wife of the senator.

Toomey, Sylvester. *The Titan.* A Chicago land agent who acts for Frank Cowperwood.

Trask, Davis. *The Titan.* A Chicago hardware prince; he owns one of the city's greatest art collections.

Trent, Kathryn. *The Stoic.* See Fleming, Berenice.

Trine, Doris. *An American Tragedy.* A clerk in a Kansas City department store; she is a friend of Hortense Briggs.

Tripp, Guy E. *The Financier.* The manager of the Delaware Navigation Company in Philadelphia; he sits on the jury trying Frank Cowperwood for embezzlement in 1871.

Trove, Charles. *An American Tragedy.* A friend of Hortense Briggs and romantic rival to Clyde Griffiths.

Troescher, John W. *An American Tragedy.* The stationmaster at Fonda, New York; at Clyde Griffiths' trial he testifies to selling Roberta Alden a ticket to Utica.

Truesdale, Mrs. *An American Tragedy.* The housekeeper for the Samuel Griffiths family in Lycurgus, New York.

Trumbull, Douglas. *An American Tragedy.* A Lycurgus, New York, attorney; he is a widower, with three children.

Trumbull, Gertrude. *An American Tragedy,* The younger daughter of Douglas Trumbull.

Trumbull, Jill. *An American Tragedy.* A friend of Sondra Finchley in Lycurgus; Clyde Griffiths is invited to attend a Christmas party at her home, and does so in the expectation of meeting Sondra there.

Trumbull, Tracy. *An American Tragedy.* The son of Douglas Trumbull; he is a law student.

Tuckerman, Ethel. *The Titan.* A member of Chicago's Garrick Players; she is the mistress of Lane Cross.

Ulrica. "Fulfilment." The actress-heroine of the story; she is indifferent to her millionaire husband and can think only of the loss of her great love, the artist Vivian, now dead.

Ungerich. *The Titan.* A political leader among the German neighborhoods in Chicago in the 1880s and 1890s.

Upham, Samuel. *An American Tragedy.* A member of the jury trying Clyde Griffiths for the murder of Roberta Alden.

Upham, Wallace. *An American Tragedy.* A resident of the Big Bittern area who reports the death of Roberta Alden to Fred Heit, the Cataraqui County Coroner.

Vance. *Sister Carrie.* A prosperous New Yorker who lives in the same apartment house as George Hurstwood and Carrie Meeber.

Vance, Mrs. *Sister Carrie.* Carrie Meeber's neighbor in New York; she takes Carrie about the city and introduces her to new shops and neighborhoods.

Vanderhoff, Wallace. *An American Tragedy.* A clerk at the Star Haberdashery in Utica, New York, who testifies that Clyde

Griffiths bought a straw hat from him.

Van Nostrand, Frederick. *The Financier.* A Philadelphian who participates in questionable financial dealings with Frank Cowperwood.

Van Ranst, Ethel. *The Bulwark.* A Smith College student, the classmate of Rhoda Walling.

Van Ranst, William. *The Bulwark.* The father of Ethel Van Ranst.

Van Rensalaer, William. "When the Old Century Was New." A New York City businessman of the year 1801.

Van Sickle, General Judson P. *The Titan.* A Chicagoan who aids Frank Cowperwood in organizing his suburban gas companies in opposition to the established utilities.

Videra. *The Titan.* A Chicago banker, the tool of Frank Cowperwood; when Stackpole seeks a loan against his stock in American Match, Cowperwood cleverly arranges for Videra to make the loan. In this manner, Cowperwood's financial enemies are prevented from knowing that he is working against their interests.

Vivian. "Fulfilment." The artist-lover of Ulrica; he dies at an early age of influenza.

Volberg, Sven. "Typhoon." A young man of the neighborhood, to whom Ida Zobel is attracted.

Waidi. "Khat"; "The Prince Who was a Thief." A water carrier in the city of Hodeidah.

Wallin, Benecia. *The Bulwark.* See Barnes, Benecia (Wallin).

Wallin, Benjamin. *The Bulwark.* An investment broker in Philadelphia; he is a first cousin of Justus Wallin.

Wallin, Cornelia. *The Bulwark.* The wife of Justus Wallin; the mother of Benecia Wallin Barnes.

Wallin, Hester. *The Bulwark.* The older sister of Justus Wallin.

Wallin, Justus. *The Bulwark.* A prosperous Quaker and Philadelphia banker, the father of Benecia Wallin Barnes.

Wallin, Segar, Jr. *The Bulwark.* A Quaker physician, related to Justus Wallin.

Wallin, Mrs. Segar, Jr. (Rhoda Kimber). *The Bulwark.* A society woman who has all but abandoned Quaker simplicity; she influences Solon Barnes' children away from their early training.

Waltham, Governor. *An American Tragedy.* The Governor of New

York; Elvira Griffiths appeals to him in a final attempt to save her son from execution.

Walton, William. *"When the Old Century Was New."* The hero of the story, a New Yorker of the year 1801.

Warburton. *The Stoic.* A London rental agent who leases Lord Stane's cottage at Pryor's Cove along the Thames to Cowperwood as a home for Berenice Fleming and her mother.

Warrington, Marsha. *The Bulwark.* A classmate of Stewart Barnes at the Red Kiln school.

Waterman, George. *The Financier.* One of the partners in the grain-commission firm in Philadelphia which gives Frank Cowperwood his first full-time employment.

Waterman, Henry, Sr. *The Financier.* A grain-commission merchant in Philadelphia who hires Frank Cowperwood when he is seventeen.

Waterman, Henry, Jr. *The Financier.* The son of Henry Waterman, Sr., and a member of the family's grain-commission business.

Watson, Dwight L. *Jennie Gerhardt.* Lester Kane's counsel in Chicago; when Lester is fatally ill, Watson brings Jennie to the Auditorium Hotel for a deathbed reconciliation.

Waxby. *"A Story of Stories."* The city editor of the *Star;* he is Augustus Binns' boss.

Wayne, Arlette. *The Stoic.* A later protégée of Frank Cowperwood; he supports her in Dresden while she studies music.

Wayne, Dr. *The Stoic.* Frank Cowperwood's physician in London; he first diagnoses the financier's illness as a fatal kidney disease.

Weaver, Otto. *Jennie Gerhardt.* A neighbor to the Gerhardt family in Columbus, Ohio; it is he who informs William Gerhardt of his daughter's affair with Senator Brander.

Webber, Richard. *The Financier.* A Philadelphia grocer selected to sit on the jury trying Frank Cowperwood for embezzlement in 1871.

Webster, Dr. *An American Tragedy.* A physician from Utica, New York, who is invited to participate in the autopsy on Roberta Alden.

Webster, Merton. *"Typhoon."* A young man to whom Ida Zobel is attracted.

Wertheim, Isaac. *The "Genius."* A New Yorker who purchases one of the paintings exhibited in Eugene Witla's first one-man show.

Westervelt, Mercedes. "Free." A classmate of Ethelberta Haymaker at the Briarcliff School.

Wheat, Skelton C. *The Financier.* A Philadelphia iron manufacturer and President of the Citizens' Municipal Reform Association; he presses for the prosecution of Frank Cowperwood in 1871.

Wheeler, Mrs. Anna. *The Stoic.* See Cowperwood, Mrs. Frank Algernon (Lillian Semple).

Wheeler, G. W. *Sister Carrie.* See Hurstwood, George W.

Wheeler, Richard. *The "Genius."* A New Yorker who serves as the Editor of *Craft* magazine, and is friendly to Eugene Witla and his work.

Whiggam, Joshua. *An American Tragedy.* A minor official at the Samuel Griffiths' shirt and collar factory in Lycurgus.

Whipple. *An American Tragedy.* The assistant to the bellboy Captain at the Green-Davidson Hotel in Kansas City while Clyde Griffiths is employed there.

Whitaker, Ada. "Nigger Jeff." A white girl who asserts that she has been assaulted by Jeff Ingalls.

Whitaker, Jake. "Nigger Jeff." The brother of Ada Whitaker; he leads a pack of vigilantes who take Jeff Ingalls from the sheriff and lynch him.

Whitaker, Morgan. "Nigger Jeff." The father of Ada Whitaker; a member of the vigilante band which lynches Jeff Ingalls.

Whitaker, Mrs. Morgan. "Nigger Jeff." The mother of Ada Whitaker.

White, Florence J. *The "Genius."* An official in Hiram Colfax's United Magazine Corporation in New York, in charge of the manufacturing and printing departments; he is Eugene Witla's chief rival for administrative supremacy in the organization.

White, Isaac. *The Titan.* A director of the North Chicago City Railway Company, which Frank Cowperwood purchases.

Whitley, Sir Wyndham. *The Stoic.* A guest aboard Lord Stane's yacht *Iola* during the cruise on which Frank Cowperwood and Berenice Fleming are passengers.

Whitmore, Norma. *The "Genius."* A writer and editor in New York; she for a time is Eugene Witla's mistress.

Whitney, Hosea. *The Financier.* A Philadelphia broker with whom Frank Cowperwood associates during the time he is working for Tighe & Co. at the stock exchange.

Whitney, Will. *Jennie Gerhardt.* A Chicago society man who makes derogatory remarks about Jennie to Lester Kane at the Union Club.

Whittridge, Mrs. *The Bulwark.* A friend to Hester Wallin.

Wiggin, David. *The Financier.* A brother of Lillian Semple Cowperwood; he is instrumental in settling the estate of Lillian's deceased husband, Alfred Semple.

Wilde, Duer. "Married." A youthful and talented pianist who marries a narrow and conventional woman.

Wilde, Marjorie. "Married." A conventional woman who finds herself ill at ease in the free and sophisticated circles frequented by her musician husband.

Wilkerson, Wilton B. *The Bulwark.* A Philadelphia carpet manufacturer; he serves as a director of the Traders and Builders Bank, in which Solon Barnes has a substantial interest.

Wilkins, Orville. *Fine Furniture.* A fireman on a donkey engine in the logging crew at Red Ledge; he is a friend of Clem Broderson.

Willets, Whydham. *The Stoic.* A major shareholder in the Deptford and Bromley subway line in London.

Williams. *The Stoic.* A maid in service to Aileen Cowperwood during her visit to London and Paris in 1900.

Williams, Barton. "The Second Choice." The phlegmatic suitor of Shirley; when she learns she cannot have her first choice, Arthur Bristow, she returns to Barton.

Williams, Caleb. *The "Genius."* The editor of the *Morning Appeal* in Alexandria, Illinois; he advises Eugene Witla to go to Chicago and attend art school.

Wilson, Grover. *An American Tragedy.* A buyer for Stark and Company; he is the uncle of Clyde Griffiths' friend Walter Dillard.

Wilson, Mrs. Norman (Carlotta Hibberdell). *The "Genius."* The daughter of Eugene Witla's landlady in Riverwood, New York; she becomes Eugene's mistress.

Wilcox, C. B. *An American Tragedy.* A neighbor to the Titus Aldens in the Biltz, New York, area; Clyde Griffiths uses the Wilcox telephone in order to place calls to Roberta Alden.

Wilcox, Ethel. *An American Tragedy.* The daughter of C.B. Wilcox; at Clyde Griffiths' trial she testifies regarding her knowledge of Roberta Alden's predicament.

Willets, Dr. *The "Genius."* An obstetrical surgeon who attends Angela Blue Witla in childbirth.

Winfield, Kenyon E. *The "Genius."* An ex-Senator from Brooklyn; a real estate plunger, Kenyon persuades Eugene Witla to invest $50,000 in his Sea Island Development Company.

Wingate, Stephen. *The Financier.* A minor Philadelphia broker who is engaged by Frank Cowperwood to become his silent partner while he is in prison in order that his business career may continue undiminished.

Winpenny. *The Financier.* A member of a delegation, including also Jacob Harmon and Edward Strobik; they visit the Governor of Pennyslvania in order to appeal directly for Frank Cowperwood's pardon.

Withers. *Sister Carrie.* The manager of the Wellington Hotel in New York; he offers Carrie Meeber a special rate for lodging in return for the prestige of her name after she has achieved fame on the stage.

Witla, Eugene Thompson. *The "Genius."* The artist-hero of the novel; he rises from obscurity to fame in the magazine-editing and arts fields. During his romance with Charlotte Wilson, he assumes the alias of Henry Kingsland in order to facilitate correspondence with her.

Witla, Myrtle. *The "Genius."* See Bangs, Mrs. Frank (Myrtle Witla).

Witla, Sylvia. *The "Genius."* See Burgess, Mrs. Benjamin (Sylvia Witla).

Witla, Thomas Jefferson. *The "Genius."* An agent for a sewing-machine company, resident of Alexandria, Illinois.

Witla, Mrs. Thomas Jefferson (Miriam). *The "Genius."* The mother of Eugene Witla.

Woodruff, William. *The Financier.* A clerk with Waterman & Co., Frank Cowperwood's first employer in Philadelphia.

Woods, William "Willie." *The Bulwark.* A friend of Stewart Barnes; he is from a Trenton, New Jersey, farming family.

Wooley, Dr. Latson. *The "Genius."* The physician who treats the Dale family; Mrs. Dale calls upon him for help with Suzanne.

Woolsen, James Furnivale. *The Titan.* A Californian who proposes a new type of streetcar line for Chicago, an electric propulsion trolley.

Wotherspoon, Robert. *The Financier.* A henchman of Edward Strobik, the Philadelphia political boss. From Wotherspoon, Albert Stires hears the story that Simpson, Butler, and Mollenhauer are conniving to send Frank Cowperwood to the penitentiary; the story is spurious, but it is in this manner that

Cowperwood learns that the trio of political leaders will not work in his favor.

Wray. "Marriage—for One." The mild-mannered clerk-hero of the story, who undertakes to awaken his bride to things intellectual.

Wary, Mrs. (Bessie). "Marriage—for One." A new bride, whose husband's efforts to preserve their marriage by making her his intellectual equal produce an ultra-liberal who walks out on him.

Wray, Janet. "Marriage—for One." The daughter of Wray and his wife, whom Bessie progressively neglects as she moves into intellectual circles.

Wundt, Pastor. *Jennie Gerhardt.* The Lutheran minister at the church attended by the Gerhardt family in Columbus, Ohio.

Wycroft, Thomas. *The Financier.* A Philadelphia alderman, one of a triumvirate of politicians engaged in selling municipal contracts.

Wynant, Constance. *An American Tragedy.* The girl friend and prospective fiancee of Gilbert Griffiths in Lycurgus, New York.

Yanee, Princess. "The Prince Who Was a Thief." The daughter of Caliph Yianko I. She marries Prince Hussein.

Yearsley, Samuel. *An American Tragedy.* A farmer from Gun Lodge, New York, who testifies at Clyde Griffiths' trial that the rough road over which Roberta Alden's body was carried to Bridgeburg may have contributed to the bruises found on the corpse.

Yianko I, Caliph. "The Prince Who Was a Thief." The ruler of Baghdad and the father of Princess Yanee.

Yussuf. "The Prince Who Was a Thief." A trainer of thieves; he undertakes the education in crime of the kidnapped Prince Hussein.

Zanders, Edward "Eddie." *The Financier.* The sheriff's deputy in charge of Frank Cowperwood at his trial in 1871.

Zang, Eberhard. *The "Genius."* A Fifth Avenue art dealer who becomes interested in Eugene Witla's paintings because of Norma Whitmore's praise of them.

Zimmerman, Joseph. *The Financier.* A wealthy dry-goods dealer in

Philadelphia who lends Frank Cowperwood $25,000 during
the panic of 1871.

Zingara. "Free." An architect in New York who has been a tre-
mendous success in his field.

Zobel, Ida. "Typhoon." A young German-American girl who,
seduced and then rejected by Edward Hauptwanger, kills
him and then herself.

Zobel, William. "Typhoon." The proprietor of a paint store.

Zobel, Mrs. William. "Typhoon." The mother of Ida Zobel.